**BY THE EDITORS OF CONSUMER GUIDE®
AND FORREST M. MIMS, III**

EASY-TO-UNDERSTAND GUIDE TO

HOME COMPUTERS

All rights reserved under International and Pan American copyright conventions. Copyright® 1982 Publications International, Ltd. This publication may not be reproduced or quoted in whole or in part by mimeograph or any other printed means, or for presentation on radio or television without written permission from Louis Weber, President of Publications International, Ltd. Permission is never granted for commercial purposes. Printed in USA.

Contents

Chapter 1
What You Can Do with Your Own Computer...5

A home computer is the ultimate jack-of-all-trades — it can play games, teach your kids, analyze your finances, and more. Here's a sample—the possibilities are almost endless.

Chapter 2
Computer Hardware: The Power in the Machine...24

Hardware is all the computer parts you can see and touch—the keyboard, the video screen, and the circuitry that makes it work. Here's how all those components work together.

Cover Design: Jeff Hapner
Cover Graphics: Quicksilver Assoc. Inc.
Illustrators: Gary Gianni, Clarence Moberg
Photo Credits: Apple Computer Inc.; Atari®; Axiom Corp.; Commodore Business Machines, Inc.; Hewlett-Packard; IBM Corp.; Intel Corp. (p. 28, p. 215); Panasonic Co.; Sharp Electronics Corp.; Sinclair Research Ltd.; Tandy Corp./Radio Shack; Texas Instruments Inc.; Timex Computer Co.

Chapter 3
Software: The Key to Successful Computing ... 48

Software—called programs—is the instructions that tell the computer exactly what to do. Find out about the different types of magnetic media, and learn what software packages can do.

Chapter 4
Peripherals: Increasing Your Computer's Power ... 80

To get the data in and out of your computer efficiently, you need peripherals—add-ons like printers. Here's a look at some of the most important accessories for home computers.

Chapter 5
Choosing Your Home Computer ... 120

Which computer is right for you? The market is changing fast—this survey of popular desktop and handheld models will help you find the computer that fits your needs.

Chapter 6
The ABCs
of Programming ... 164

You don't have to know how to program a home computer to use it, but you'll see that programming is easier than you think—and it can be fun!

Chapter 7
The Future: What's
Ahead in Computers? ... 203

Computers can do a lot today, but there's even more excitement predicted for the future. Take a look at what's coming tomorrow—and the next day.

Bibliography:
Selected Periodicals ... 221

Glossary ... 226

Index ... 243

Chapter 1

How does a computer fit into your home? It can play games, teach the kids, plan menus, figure your taxes, help run your business—and that's just for starters! A home computer is both your personal problem-solver and your link to tomorrow.

What You Can Do With Your Own Computer

TO MANY PEOPLE, the word "computer" is a kind of future shock — an image of huge, intimidating machines banked in specially climate-controlled rooms, deep in corporate America. The people who use them, we think, are an elite group — far from ordinary people, hunched over their glowing video screens like sorcerers bending over a bubbling cauldron.

Is it true? No. Those machines will always have a place in business—they keep track of our taxes, send out insurance policies, figure our utility bills. But suddenly, over the past few years, a new crop of computers has sprouted. Instead of ominous, room-size boxes, these machines are friendly *personal information machines*—affordable automated servants that can help you keep track of your budget, figure your taxes, store and retrieve recipes, and even write your checks at the end of the month.

Over the past few years, hundreds of thousands of these low-cost computers have flooded the market. Today's *personal,* or *home,* computers, which often sell for well under $500, have all the power of a computer costing tens of thousands of dollars ten years ago. Today, just about anyone can buy one, take it home and plug it in—and have computer power at his or her fingertips.

WHAT IS A COMPUTER?

In the broadest sense, a personal computer is any product that contains a *microprocessor.* This technological wonder — about the size of a fingernail, and a direct outgrowth of the miniaturization achieved during the 1960s space program—contains tens of thousands of microscopic transistors, and is the real brains of a computer. Today, microprocessors can be found in many familiar products and places—in home or arcade video games, microwave ovens, automobiles, supermarket checkout registers, and all the other smart servants we've learned to take for granted.

The dictionary calls a computer an electronic device that stores, retrieves, and processes information. Well, many calculators can do that. To narrow things down a little more, think of a computer as a device that takes a set, or list, of steps called a *program* — and some information—more commonly called *data* in the computer world—and automatically works on the information to produce new data, without any help from you. The key word here is "automatically" —a handheld calculator does much the same thing a computer does, but you must manually enter each step. The computer can do some thinking for itself.

Take a look at the gadgets you depend on — you'll find computer-type brains in calculators, microwaves, and more.

They look complicated, but all computers do, essentially, four things. Whatever their size, all computers use an *input* device for getting information in, a *processor* for working on the information, *memory* to store information, and an *output* device — usually a TV-like screen — for getting the new information out to you. There's more to computers than that, of course — but once you know the basics, it's easy to understand just why computers are becoming so important.

We'll take a much closer look at how computers are physically set up in the next chapter, but two terms you should immediately become familiar with are *hardware* and *software*. These are the two most common words you'll hear when people talk about computers, and they aren't hard to define. *Hardware* is the physical components of the computer, the things you can see and touch. The keyboard, the microprocessor, the video display screen, and accessories like cassette tape recorders and printers are all examples of hardware. *Software*, on the other hand, is a set of electrical instructions that tell the computer what to do. Software isn't so tangible, but it's

The typical home computer consists of a keyboard to type information in and a video screen to display it. The computer's brains may be in a separate box, or built into the keyboard or the display.

software that's the real brains of the outfit—without it, the computer is helpless. Software normally comes on cassette tape, floppy disks, and plug-in cartridges. Don't worry about all these terms and names if you're not familiar with them; we'll cover them as we go along.

Types of Computers

There are a number of types of computers. In this book, we'll mainly concentrate on what are commonly known as *desktop* computers. It's easy to see why they got that name; they easily fit on the top of a desk. They're *personal* because only you are using the computer at any point in time—unlike the huge business computers, which hundreds of people may use at the same time. It's as simple as that—a home computer is one you can use at home.

Desktop computers usually have a typewriter-style keyboard, a main chassis that contains the actual computer electronics, and a video display screen that lets the computer communicate with you by displaying words on the screen. Some desktop computers let you use your home television as a video display; you can plug the brains right into the TV you already have. As we'll see later, most home computers have a number of *peripherals* — accessories like printers for getting a permanent copy of your computations, and cassette tape recorders or *floppy disk drives* for storing data.

A variation of the desktop computer is the *handheld* or *pocket* computer, so called because it can fit in your pocket and can be used in the palm of your hand, just like a pocket calculator. But handheld computers are more than glorified calculators. They do have a few limitations, but they're powerful computers in their own right.

Over the next few years, the line between desktop and handheld computers will become more and more hazy. Already, some companies have introduced *portable* computers, with all the power of the desktop models, packed in a take-along case the size of a sewing machine. The portables are sure to become more and more popular — in not too many years, you'll see business people on their morning commute busily using their computers as they ride to work.

Everything we'll talk about in this book applies to all these types of home computers. Just remember, a computer is a computer, whether it's in your pocket or it fills a room of its own in the headquarters of a large corporation. Today's home computers are a far cry from those room-size monsters — and you'll be surprised at all the things they can do for you.

WHAT CAN YOU DO WITH A HOME COMPUTER?

Although home computers make the power of computers available to just about anyone, they're still a substantial investment. You can get a basic computer for less than $100, spend $300 to $500 for a medium-range model, or spend $1,000 or even $5,000 for an advanced system designed for professional or business use. Why do you need a home computer, and what can one of these machines do for you? The answer is simple: personal computers are the ultimate jack-of-all-trades, and can replace pencils, paper, chalkboards, typewriters, filing cabinets, and address books. They can do more than that, too — they're your link to the future, to the high-tech global world of tomorrow. In the next few pages, we'll try to give you an overview of the wide and wonderful world of home computers and why you may want to make one part of your life — now.

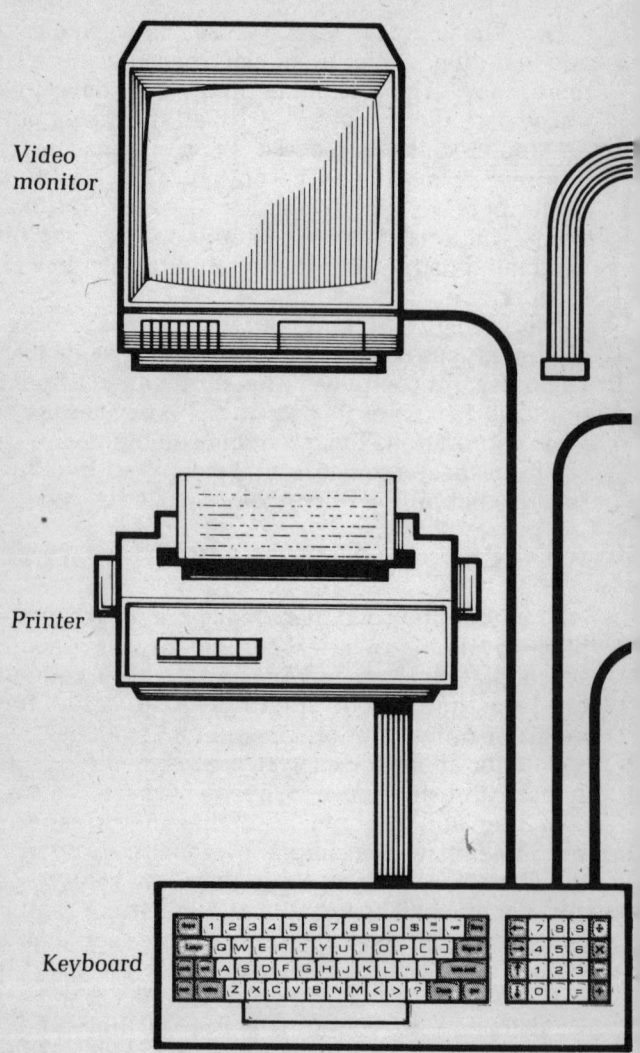

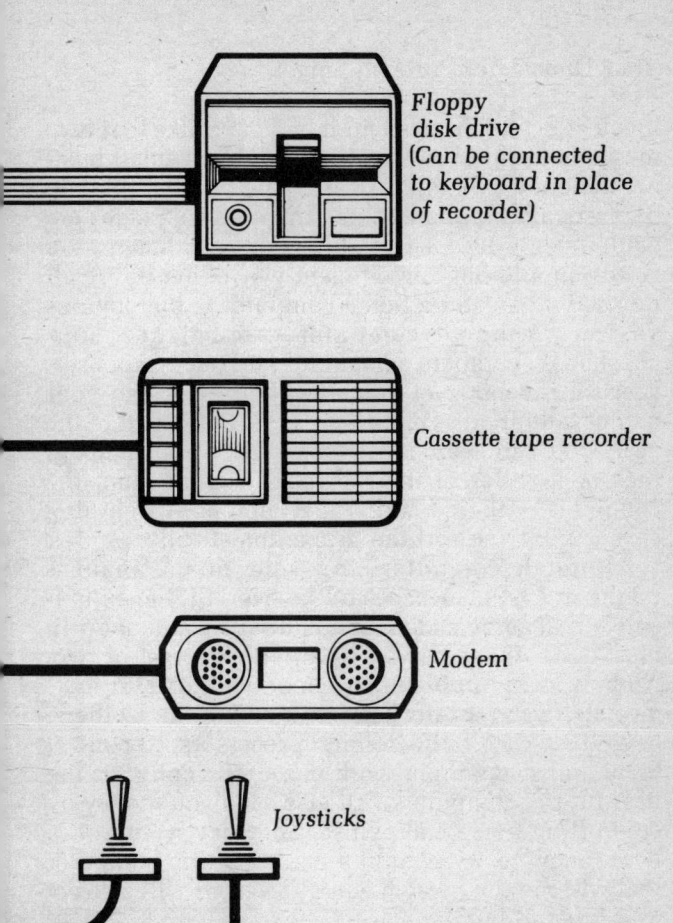

Floppy disk drive (Can be connected to keyboard in place of recorder)

Cassette tape recorder

Modem

Joysticks

A computer system often includes accessories called peripherals. The keyboard here contains the brains; everything else is plugged in—the video monitor and printer to get information out, the joysticks to put it in, the disk drive and other devices to move information both ways.

Your Household Problem-Solver

If you stop and think about it, you'll realize that running a household is a lot like running a small business. Money is brought in and paid out; equipment, like cars and appliances, is "invested in"; taxes are paid; inventories are kept. Like any good business, a family should have an efficient way of managing all this activity — and a home computer is the obvious answer. A home computer can balance your checkbook, compare actual and budgeted expenses, keep an inventory of groceries, help you plan your menus, and figure Uncle Sam's bite at the end of the year. You can keep an updated list of your belongings or a roster of the members of your club; the computer will find individual entries at lightning speed, and even sort the lists automatically.

Although computerizing your home finances might, at first glance, seem like overkill, the end result is that a home computer can save you money. In most cases, it can pay for itself within a year or two. Already many appliances, such as automatic thermostats, water heaters, electric stoves, and others, have their own built-in microprocessors, to control them and make them work more efficiently. In the near future, computers will also save you money by controlling home energy use. Someday, your entire home may be wired into a central home computer that will not only watch energy use, but will also act as a fire and burglar alarm.

Your Personal Investment Counselor

You can use a home computer to quickly look at investment options to see what you could earn by investing your money, from banks to money market funds. Sure, a pocket calculator can do that too, but you'd need lots of notes and a great deal of time. The computer does away with all that, displaying on a video screen a well-organized comparison of investment plans. And it can also do complicated analyses that would take hours if you used a pocket calculator.

Other home computer users get up-to-the-minute reports on stocks and bonds by hooking their computers up to computer information utilities — the Dow Jones News/Retrieval service, for instance — through the telephone lines. A home computer can get you all the information you need, spot trends, and make investment suggestions, for the kind of financial guidance only the pros could give you a few years ago.

Education: Your Personal Tutor

The educational possibilities of home computers — for both kids and adults — are almost unlimited. More and more schools are teaching *computer literacy*—and the kids are taking to the computers with none of the technical timidity that plagues many adults. Special educational software is widely available to give children a head start on their schoolwork and reinforce the learning process later on. And just watch any 10-year-old at a video arcade!

The involvement of the video games is what makes them work, and home computers work for education for the same reason — they make students get involved. In addition to reading a book or listening to a teacher, children can use home computers as personal tutors, leading them step by step through a subject, and letting them learn at an individual pace. Many educational programs designed for kids use an electronic-game format to keep the kids interested and alert. Fast action, coupled with lots of colorful

Kids learn fast and stay interested with the computer's electronic teaching. Even multiplication can be fun!

graphics and sound effects, can keep even the most reluctant learner involved and interested.

These electronic tutors have already found a place in the schools; more and more school systems are making computer education mandatory. And a computer at home to go along with the school's system can speed up the learning process even more.

But adults aren't left out, either. Advanced educational software is becoming available all the way up through post-college level — a boon to busy homemakers and professionals. Want to learn a foreign language, advanced math, or electronics theory? Your own home computer can help you.

Games

A look at what a home computer can do wouldn't be complete without the games. Many people buy home computers especially to play games, but soon find other more useful applications for their home com-

Today's computers can display charts and graphs in full color, either on a video monitor or on your own TV.

puter. Whatever your background, games are a terrific introduction to the world of computers.

Hundreds of games are available for most home computers. Most games are much more colorful and advanced than those available with home video game systems that plug into a television set. In fact, many come close to the excitement of realism of arcade games. Best of all, you don't have to leave home — and you don't have to put in a quarter to play.

The Business Arena

Many personal computers are specifically designed for business use—and "business" doesn't just mean top executives. Today, whether you run a small business at home, you're a professional such as a doctor or dentist, or you manage a small company you'll find that a personal computer can save precious time and money, and keep better track of things. And that's worth looking into, for any business.

If you visit a computer store, you'll see more computer systems and programs designed for business purposes than for any other application. Although *any* personal computer can be used in business, some are specifically designed for it; they have extra memory, larger keyboards, special video displays, and many other features. Of course, all those extras do cost more — but if you want to use a personal computer for business, the price is probably worth it. Before you buy a home computer, be sure to take a look at the systems designed for business.

Word Processing

One of the most popular business uses of computers — and one that can also be very useful for individuals—is word processing. "You, Mr. and Mrs. Jones, may be a winner in our grand sweepstakes. In the near future, you could be receiving a check for one million dollars at 31 Fireside Lane." How many times have you received such a "personal" letter from a mail-order firm, credit card company, magazine publisher, or politician? These letters were typed by computers that automatically inserted your name, address, and other personal information at the right place in the letter. The same letter—with other people's names and addresses — probably went to hundreds of thousands of others.

This type of mailing is just one example of one of the handiest things a home computer can do. It's called *word processing*, and it allows you to use a computer as an advanced typewriter, with the video display as your "electronic paper." Word processing is not just a business technology — it can be done with nearly any personal computer, with programs designed for the purpose.

Although you might ask what advantage there is to seeing your words on the screen—you still have to have a printer to make a final typewritten copy — word processing has many advantages. You can move words, phrases, sentences, and paragraphs around, putting them exactly where you want them. You can even take out whole sections — the spaces automatically close up. When your letter or report is in exactly the form you want it, you press a button and print it out on paper. Not a bad way to write a term paper! You can even do your own personalized letters to a long list of people, or send an up-to-the-minute newsletter to everyone in the family.

Don't know how to type? Don't worry! There are even programs that teach touch-typing, and programs that check your spelling by comparing all the words you've typed with the entries in an electronic dictionary. Soon there will even be programs that check your grammar.

Using a home computer as a word processor is a valuable time-saver, even if you just type occasional letters or reports. And if you do lots of writing—as your job or as part of your job—you'll never look back once you've experienced the convenience of computer-age word processing.

Your Window on the World

All this is impressive, but home computers can do much more than specific tasks. They can also broaden your horizons, by letting you obtain information on an almost unlimited number of subjects. By hooking your home computer to a telephone line using a special accessory box called a *modem*, you can explore the wide world of *telecomputing* — linking your computer to huge computer *databases* located all over the United States. Besides the investment information we talked about earlier, computer information services such as The Source and CompuServe let you get the latest news and weather, exchange *electronic mail*—like talking to CB or ham radio operators—with other computer users all over the country, and even make travel reservations from the comfort of your home. You can even browse through nationwide classified ads and do your mail-order shopping with a home computer.

Is it expensive? After a registration fee—perhaps $100—most of these services cost about $5 to $20 an hour, depending on the time of day you use the service. And in that period of time you can get more information than you know what to do with. There usually isn't even a long-distance telephone charge. Because the companies that maintain these data-

A modem lets you hook your home computer into a telephone line — computers all over the country can "talk" together.

bases have telephone lines all over the country, hooking into these "information depositories" is a simple matter of making a local phone call from most metropolitan areas and giving the information service's computer your personal password.

And Lots More

As you can see, the list of what a home computer can do for you is virtually endless. If you've heard about these machines but have been afraid to get involved, fear not! Today's home computers are "user-friendly"—they lead you step by step through their operation. You don't even have to learn how to program a computer, although many people do learn because it's fun. Commercial ready-to-run software is available for all the purposes we've talked about, and many more. All you do is plug the programs in — we'll see how later in this book — push a button, and off you go!

LEARNING MORE ABOUT COMPUTERS

If you've read this far, you're already interested in becoming a part of the home computer revolution. The first step in getting involved is educating yourself. This book is designed to give you a background in home computers that will let you hold your own when you enter a computer store.

Plenty of additional information is available from other sources, too. Subscribe to computer magazines —a selected list of periodicals is included at the back of this book. Join a local computer club or users' group. Get to know people who own and operate home computers, and send for information and brochures from computer manufacturers. Many colleges and even some computer stores offer excellent computer courses designed for beginners. Besides introductory courses, which can be found all over the country, there are many more specialized courses on hardware and basic programming. You might even want to make computers your career — it's a great field to get into.

Another way to learn about personal computers is to use them. Nothing beats hands-on experience, and it's a great way to get an idea of which computer is best for you. Any computer store should be glad to give you the chance to try out various computers. Give it a chance!

There are even computer camps designed to get you up and running on computers. Although the first camps were designed for children only, adult camps are beginning to spring up all over the country. They can be a great way to combine a relaxing vacation and some practical education at the same time.

The Future Is Now

It hasn't taken long; computers are here — and the best advice we can offer is for you to get involved with home computers *now*. Jump in with both feet; the future is waiting — and your knowledge of computers will give you valuable experience for the way we'll live in the years ahead. It might be a little confusing at first, but the confusion won't last long once you get started. Computers are already here — whether you realize it or not, they're already a big part of your life. Don't wait to take advantage of the future—the world of computers is too good to miss.

Chapter 2

What is hardware, and how does it work? How can a machine have a memory? How do all the pieces work together? Computerese isn't as complicated as it sounds—once you know the basics, you'll talk computer language like a pro.

Computer Hardware: The Power in the Machine

IF YOU'VE VISITED a store that sells computers or have friends who are involved with computers, you're probably confused by all the jargon you've been hearing. Terms like "hardware," "software," "operating systems," "RAM," "ROM," and many others are always being thrown around by people in the know. Well, the world of computers has its own special language, just like many other fields. We'll try to keep the jargon to a minimum, but it's important for you to understand some of these terms. And so you can make an intelligent buying decision and hold your own with computer people, you're going to have to learn a little about how computers tick.

HARDWARE VS. SOFTWARE

The two most common terms you'll hear are "hardware" and "software"—basically, the machinery and the brains. Hardware and software are the two essential aspects of computers, and the difference between them is important. We're going to devote a full chapter to each, to explain exactly what the terms mean and why they're important; and along the way we'll tell you a little about how a computer works. Software is discussed in the next chapter; this chapter is about the machinery itself—the hardware.

One of the dictionary definitions of hardware is that it's the physical part of an electrical or electronic device. That's exactly what computer hardware is: the electronic circuitry, video display, case, disk drives, and other components you can touch. (We'll define all these terms as we go along.) In other words, hardware is comprised of the tangible parts of your computer system, the parts you can physically hold. You might even think of a store that sells computers as a sort of hardware store. Software is another area altogether, and we'll go into it in detail in Chapter 3, "Software: The Key to Successful Computing." For now, think of software as a series of instructions in the form of electrical signals that tell your computer what to do.

Your home computer is basically made up of four separate sections: the microprocessor, the memory, input, and output. Regardless of a computer's size or power—whether it's the largest *mainframe* machine that's kept in a specially built and controlled environment or the small handheld *microcomputer*—all do essentially the same thing. All computers have an input device, like a keyboard, for getting information in; a processor for working on the information; a memory to store information; and an output device, like a video display screen, for getting the new information out to you.

Hardware is every part of the computer system that you can touch—keyboard, video screen, and accessories.

Another type of hardware is peripherals, basically any accessory that is, to some degree, controlled by the computer. These devices are discussed in Chapter 4, "Peripherals: Increasing Your Computer's Power."

THE MICROPROCESSOR

The microprocessor is the brains of your computer. Without it, there would be no home computer revolution. Although the term "computer" is used to describe your entire system, the microprocessor is the

The microprocessor chip, so tiny it's dwarfed by a daisy, is the real brains of the computer. It's made of silicon, and etched with thousands of electronic circuits — the transistors that actually do the computing.

electronic part that actually does the computing. What's mind-boggling is that all this power is on a tiny chip of silicon made from purified beach sand, no bigger than the nail on your index finger. Etched on this chip is a complicated maze of tens of thousands of microscopic transistors that can work at blinding speed — millions of times per second.

Many people are surprised to find that the microprocessor only understands two things: the digits 0 and 1. This two-digit language is called the binary numbering system. The microprocessor gets all of its information in a continuous stream of bits (short for binary digit) that register data according to whether there's voltage present (a 1) or no voltage (a 0).

Explaining exactly how your computer's microprocessor works is much too technical to discuss here, and it isn't really necessary for you to know this to use a computer. But you should be aware that there are a number of different brands of microprocessor chips. As you venture further into the world of home computers, you'll probably hear about the pros and cons of each one. But despite the different names and model numbers, Z-80 and 6502 are the names you'll probably hear most commonly; the Z-80 microprocessor is by far the most popular. Microprocessors are very much alike — they all do essentially the same thing. The name of the microprocessor is not a major concern.

Another thing you're sure to hear about is the number of bits a microprocessor has. This refers to how large a chunk of information — more often called *data* — a microprocessor chip can handle at one time. Remember that each bit is either a 1 or a 0 in the binary number system? Well, if a microprocessor handled information a single bit at a time, it would take an awfully long time for it to do even a simple task. Early models of microprocessors handled information in 4-bit chunks, but for various technical reasons, their usefulness was limited. The 8-bit microprocessor, developed several years ago, is now the industry standard; you'll find an 8-bit microprocessor in the vast majority of today's home computers. That 8-bit chunk of data, by the way, brings us to another term you'll hear a lot about—a byte. In computerese, a byte is eight bits. Four bits is —you guessed it—a nibble.

In the near future, you're going to be hearing more and more about 16-bit microprocessors. They're just now beginning to become available for some personal computers. But so far, computers that use them

Microprocessors handle information in units called bytes. A byte is a chunk of eight bits—the binary digits 0 and 1. Most home computers use one-byte microprocessors, but some have microprocessors that can take two bytes at a time.

are quite a bit more expensive than computers that use 8-bit microprocessors. These 16-bit microprocessors have two big advantages: They're a lot faster than 8-bit chips, and they can handle more memory. But there's one disadvantage, too — 16-bit microprocessors require special programs, and there are very few of these programs around at the present time. If you're going to be using your computer on a day-to-day basis for an important job, like running a business, it will be well worth your while to take a look at a computer that uses a 16-bit microprocessor.

MEMORY

Although the microprocessor is probably the essential component, all the separate parts of your computer would be useless by themselves—they must all work together to make a working computer. Memory is another important area, and one where you're likely to hear a lot of confusing and conflicting information. Your computer's microprocessor must get the information it works on — the software — from somewhere and it has to store the results of its computations, too. That's where memory comes in.

If you could see through the cabinet protecting your computer, you'd see an array of chips—the tiny black boxes that hold the microscopic circuitry. The largest box is usually the microprocessor, but there are other chips too, normally lined up in a row. This is the computer's internal memory. In each of the chips are thousands of simple on/off switches, which are used to store binary information—on for 1, off for 0. Those thousands of switch combinations are the actual program that the microprocessor works on. We'll give you an in-depth explanation of programs and software in Chapter 3.

Actually, there are three types of computer memory. There's random-access memory (RAM), which, like an electronic scratch pad, handles the instructions you give the computer and can be later erased. There's also read-only memory (ROM), which contains permanently stored instructions that a computer requires to do its basic, routine operations. The third type of computer memory is some external means of storing information you want to save. This is done with cassette tapes or floppy disks, and is explained later in this chapter.

RAM: The Electronic Scratch Pad

The memory the computer uses to obey the instructions you give it is called RAM, or random-access memory, and it's a term you'll run into again and again as you continue to explore the world of computers. Actually, however, RAM is a misnomer. A better name might be read/write memory because information can either be read from the RAM or put into it—*written to* the ram—by electrically changing those microscopic switches from on to off, or vice versa. Writing to RAM is done when you put into the computer—or *load*—a program. The microprocessor also writes to the RAM after it's finished with its computations.

Because RAM can be confusing, it might be helpful to think of it as a series of post office boxes. At any given point in time, an individual box might or might not have information (mail) in it. If you consider an empty post office box to be a 0 and a full post office box to be a 1, you'll get an idea of how RAM works.

One of the most important things to remember about RAM is that when you turn the computer off, all the information that's stored in these chips is lost because these chips require electrical current to retain information. That's why storing programs in external forms of memory, as explained below, is so important. Memory that loses its information is called *volatile* memory. We'll talk about *nonvolatile* memory shortly.

How Much RAM Is Enough? As if things weren't complicated enough, you'll also have to consider how much RAM you need. Most ready-to-run software packages — also called "canned" programs — require quite a bit of memory, and if your computer doesn't have enough memory, you can't run the program. How much memory is enough? Well, there are a few standard sizes.

The standard measure of computer memory size is a "K." In many fields, that stands for an even 1,000; it's taken from the prefix "kilo-," 1,000. But in computers, a K is 1,024 bytes — and a byte is an 8-bit chunk, eight individual microscopic on/off switches. Why a byte instead of bits? It's just that it's much handier to think of it in that way, because the computer handles the data in 8-bit groups anyway.

The most common memory size for home computers is 16K RAM—that's 16,384 bytes. Although that might sound like a lot, it doesn't take long for a relatively short computer program to fill them up. To give you an idea of how much space 16K is, consider how long this book would be in the binary system. If you took only four of these pages and turned each letter, number, punctuation mark, and space — even spaces need a memory location — into the binary code of 1s and 0s the computer works with, it would easily fill 16K of memory.

Adding Memory. Some computers come with only 4K RAM of memory, but it's generally a good idea to stay away from them, because the programs they'll be able to run are limited. The minimum RAM memory you should have is 16K. Fortunately, most home

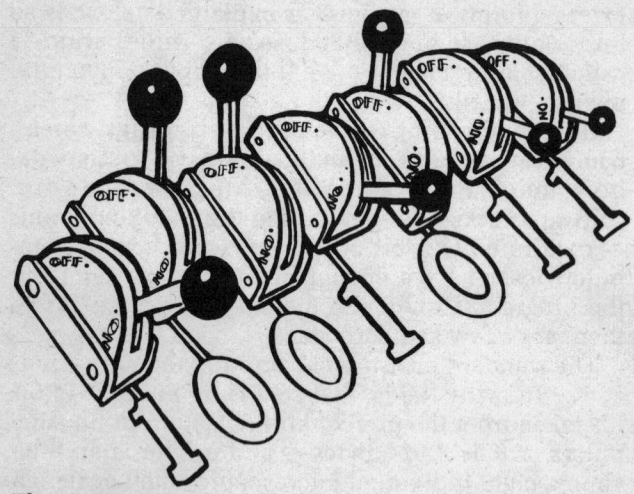

The computer's internal memory consists of chips that contain thousands of microscopic on/off switches. The switches store binary information—the computer reads 0 when a switch is off, and 1 when it's on. The combination of 0s and 1s tells the computer what to do.

computers allow you to add additional memory later on. In some cases it's a simple matter of plugging in a circuit board; in others you have to return your computer to a service center to have the new circuits added. We'll talk about this in Chapter 4, "Peripherals: Increasing Your Computer's Power."

Many of today's small home computers can handle up to 64K of RAM. Adding this much memory to your computer will cost a couple of hundred extra dollars, but if you're serious about using your computer it's a good investment. Be aware, too, that some advanced programs may need a full 64K of RAM.

What about more than 64K? Most home computers

won't take any more than this, because that's all the memory their microprocessors can handle. Some of the new 16-bit microprocessors can handle 256K or even 512K of RAM, but there's little software currently available that can take advantage of all this memory space. When it does become available, the first programs for computers with 16-bit microprocessors will probably be designed for sophis-

Some computers come with only 4K of RAM memory, but you should have at least 16K. You can also add memory—sometimes up to 64K.

ticated business machines — not for home computers.

ROM: Internal Operating Instructions

The other common type of memory contained in every small home computer is ROM, which stands for read-only memory — the built-in operating instructions used by the computer. As you might guess by the name, information can only be read from the

The computer's ROM memory holds its internal instructions — the start-up procedures that get it operating when you turn it on.

ROM — not written to it. ROMs are memory chips that have their microscopic on/off switches permanently set at the factory when they're manufactured; you can never alter the information in the computer's ROM, as you do its RAM. ROM is *nonvolatile memory*; it can't be lost if you turn off the power to the computer. Although many manufacturers tell you how much ROM they have installed in their computers—the amount is measured in "K," just as with RAM—this isn't an important buying consideration.

There are several good reasons why your computer needs ROMs. The first is that every time you turn on the computer, it must be told how to start itself up. Most home computers go through a number of automatic checks to make sure all circuits are in top operating shape. These start-up and check-up operations are built-in programs, often called *bootstrap* programs because the computer gets itself into an operating condition by "pulling itself up by the bootstraps."

Nearly every home computer also comes with a high-level computer programming language called BASIC built in, so you can easily communicate with the computer. Because the computer needs to know BASIC to understand what you feed into it, it's most convenient to store this knowledge permanently in the computer's ROM chips. That way, you don't have to waste time reprogramming the computer to understand BASIC—loading it from a cassette tape or a floppy disk—every time you want to use the computer.

INPUT DEVICES

Without a way to get information both into and out of your computer, your machine would be very much like a human brain without any of the five senses — potentially smart, but practically helpless. Input is putting information in, and there are several ways of doing this.

The Keyboard

The most common device for inputting information to a computer is a typewriter-like keyboard. The keyboard lets you give instructions to the computer.

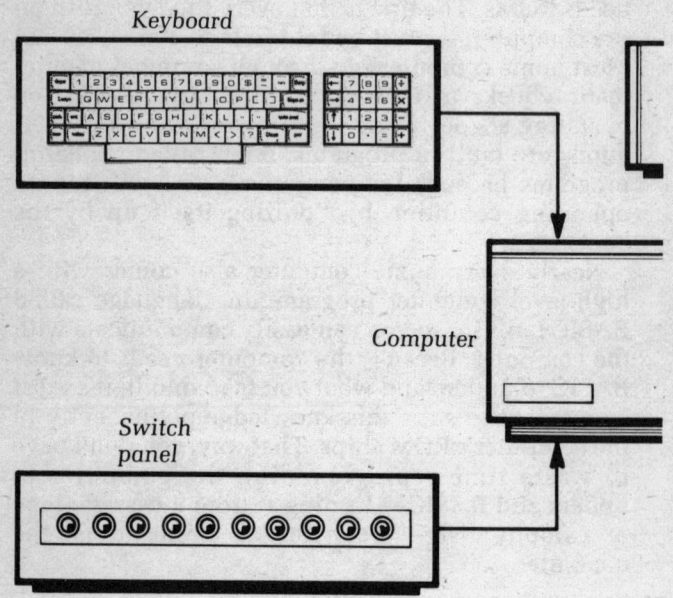

Every time you press a key, a special binary code consisting of a special combination of voltage/no-voltage pulses — 1s and 0s — is generated. The microprocessor chip interprets your instructions and acts on them.

If you look closely at the keyboard of most home computers, you'll see that besides the normal letter,

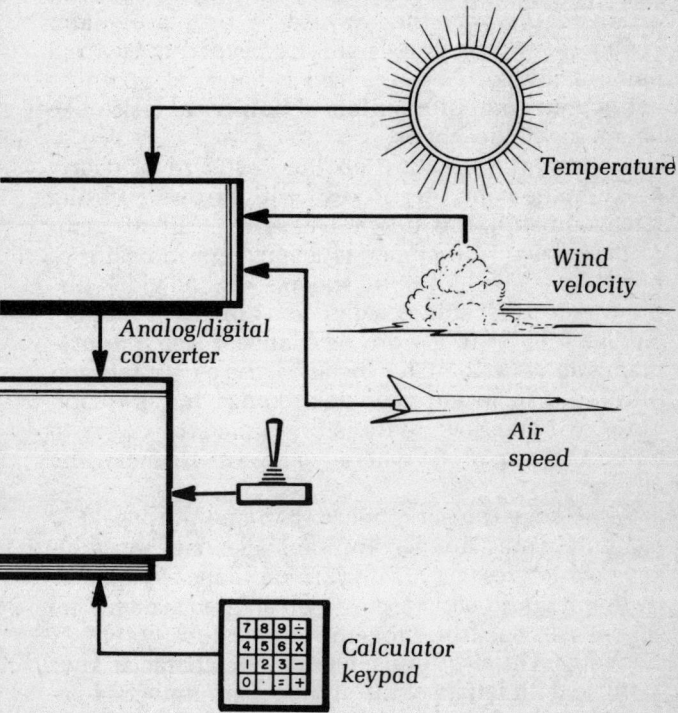

Input doesn't have to be just through the keyboard. You can also feed information in through a calculator keypad, a joystick, or even a switch board. An analog/digital converter converts variable information, like temperature, into signals the computer understands.

number, and punctuation keys, there are often other keys marked with such terms as "Escape," "Break," and "Control." These keys produce special codes that tell your computer to perform certain tasks. For example, the "Break" key tells the microprocessor to stop what it's doing and wait for further instructions from the keyboard. In addition, many keyboards have a separate numeric *keypad*, with numbers arranged the way they would be on a calculator keyboard. Although a calculator keypad is far from being a necessity, you'll find it handy if you'll be using your computer for lots of numerical tasks, like balancing a checkbook.

An important feature on the keyboard of nearly every home computer is keys with arrows pointing left, right, up, and down. These are called *cursor control keys*. The cursor is a movable indicator — normally a small blinking square—on the video display screen that shows where you are. If you want to change a letter in a word or change a line in a program you've written, for instance, the cursor lets you pinpoint the location of this change for the computer. All you have to do is press the arrow keys to move the cursor to where you want to make the change.

Some keys can serve more than one purpose. For example, many home computers also have graphics keys, which let you create various shapes—squares, rectangles, and other forms—on a video screen. The shapes can be strung together to produce graphs or drawings. On most home computers, character keys —those with letters of the alphabet or numbers—are also the graphics keys. By giving the computer a command, these letter or number keys can be shifted into their graphics mode, much like depressing the "shift" key on an ordinary typewriter to produce uppercase letters.

Graphics keys turn your computer into an electronic pallette—you can create original art, and even pictures that move.

Other Input Devices

Although a keyboard is the most commonly used way of giving a home computer instructions, there are other ways. If you'll be using your computer to play some of the fast-action video games, you'll probably be using a joystick—a box with a lever that moves in all directions, something like the control stick used in an airplane. Like the controls used in some arcade games, joysticks let you move a spacecraft or some other object on the video screen fast enough to shoot down alien invaders, and save the world for truth, justice, and the American way. Joysticks are usually a low-cost option that plugs right into your computer.

There are also some special-purpose input devices that you may hear about, although you probably won't become involved with them. These are called analog/digital converters, or A/D converters for short. A/D converters measure things like room temperature and convert it into the binary signals—0s and 1s — a computer understands. The uses of such converters are only now beginning to be explored. Someday in the not too far distant future, your home computer will use these A/D converters to control the environment of your home.

Another far-out input device, now still in the experimental stage, is voice recognition circuitry. Someday, you'll be able to give instructions to your computer by just speaking to it. Developing a system to do something like this sounds complicated—and it is! Expensive voice recognition systems that hook up to sophisticated computers are available now, but so far they'll only understand a few words.

OUTPUT DEVICES

Now that we've looked briefly at what goes on inside a computer and the keyboard for communicating to the computer, the next obvious question is, how does the computer get the information to the outside world? This is where output devices come in.

The Video Display

The most common output device is the video display tube (VDT), also known as the video monitor or cathode-ray tube (CRT). Video displays, in the strict sense of the term, are television sets without the ability to tune in channels. But many home computers let you use your home color or black-and-white television set as a video display. This is done by using special circuitry—an RF modulator—that converts the computer's output to a TV channel so you can tune it in just like the late movie. The RF modulator may be built into the computer or may consist of a small box that attaches to the TV set. RF modulators are used with home video game systems. A high-quality monitor can cost more than your computer, so using your television set as a video monitor for your computer can save you quite a bit of money. But there are some disadvantages. Besides the possible fight over who in the family gets to use the home TV, a standard television set just doesn't provide as good a picture as a video monitor specially designed for use with computers can. That's not a problem for occasional use or video games, but if you'll be using your computer for word processing — producing printed correspondence or reports — you'll have a problem seeing small letters on the TV set's screen.

Whether a home computer shows color on the video display depends first on whether its circuitry can produce a color picture. If it can, you can use either a color or a black-and-white video display. Many of today's home computers produce a color picture; you can't beat it for games and entertainment uses.

Color, however, isn't a necessity for making a computer useful. In fact, most of the more expensive

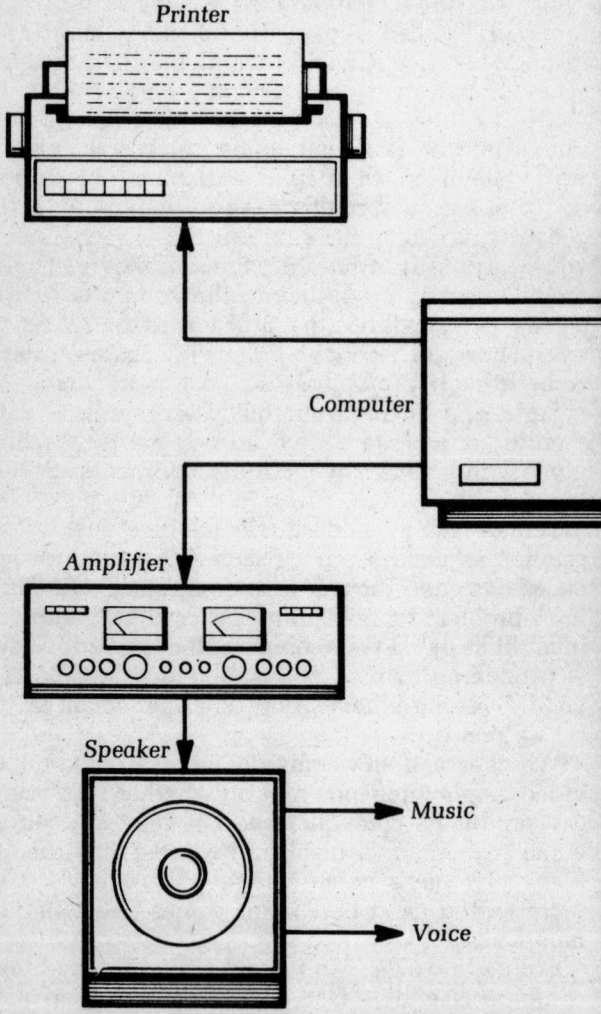

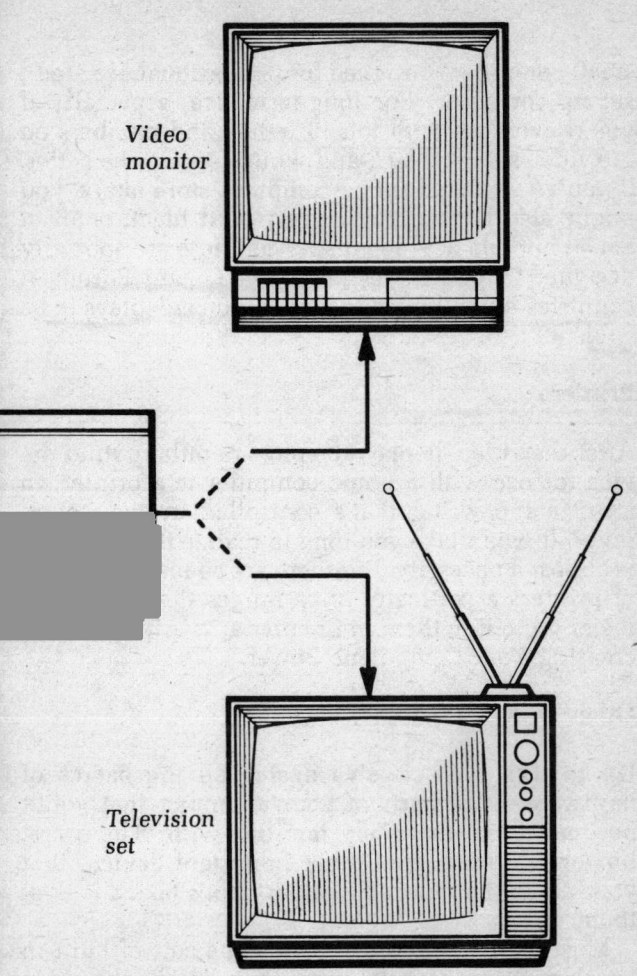

To get information out of the computer, you need output. The most common output device is the video display — either a special video monitor or your own TV. You can also get written output, with a printer — or audio output, with an amplifier and speaker.

small computers designed for professional use aren't set up for color. For long-term use, especially if you're working with lots of letters and numbers on the video screen, black-and-white seems to be better. If you've ventured into a computer store lately, you might also have noticed green and black or even amber and black video displays. These are specially designed to reduce eyestrain. In fact, many European countries will allow only amber video displays to be sold.

Printers

After the video display, the most popular output device for use with a home computer is a printer, in effect a typewriter that's controlled by your computer. It won't take you long to realize that a printer is almost a necessity. But there are so many varieties of printers at so many price ranges that we give a major section to them in Chapter 4, "Peripherals: Increasing Your Computer's Power."

Other Output Devices

Up to this point, we've described the basics of hardware — the parts of your computer that you'll become most intimately familiar with. There are, however, a number of other important devices that your computer can send data to. Let's take a look at them.

Most home computers have some sort of built-in speaker. Some do little more than beep; others can play some pretty sophisticated music. What comes out of the computer's speaker depends on the software you use, the program that actually tells your computer what to do. Most home computers allow you to program it to play some rudimentary music—

one tone at a time. In addition, if you own a stereo system, you can often connect your computer to it and play computer music through your system's large speakers or record it. There's no stereo sound yet, but this will probably come too — the digital recordings now available are achieved through the use of computers.

Some computers will even talk to you—shades of *2001: A Space Odyssey*! Voice synthesis is a growing part of computer science. Although getting a computer to speak isn't anywhere near as complicated as getting it to listen—the voice recognition circuitry we talked about earlier—it's still complicated, because human speech is made up of many complicated tones. Once again, there's software available for some home computers that will program your computer to speak. Right now, the sound is more than a little tinny. So don't expect the casual, polished tones of HAL, the computer in *2001*.

INPUT/OUTPUT DEVICES

Although it's convenient to lump computer hardware into input and output categories, there are some devices that are actually *both* input and output devices. Floppy disk drives, cassette tape recorders, and modems all fit into this category, because they both feed information into the computer and take information out. *Terminals* are a special kind of input/output device and are essentially a keyboard and a video display.

Chapter 3

Computer software comes in different forms, but it all does the same thing—it's the instructions, called programs, that tell the computer what to do. And you'll be amazed at how much all this software can do for you!

Software: The Key to Successful Computing

IF YOU READ computer ads or visit a computer store, you're sure to come across the terms "hardware" and "software." They're the most basic elements of computer jargon. You know that hardware is the parts of the computer that you can see and touch—the keyboard, a video display screen, and complex electronic circuitry concealed behind a cabinet. But there's much more to the computer than that. You also need software—the electrical instructions, or programs, that tell the computer exactly what to do. Without software, a home computer is nothing but a useless collection of hardware.

To better understand the distinction between hardware and software, consider a recipe for baking a cake. The cake recipe in the cookbook is a specific list of instructions—a program—that tells you how to make the cake, using the ingredients — the "hardware."

Computer software tells your computer how to do specific tasks: balancing your checkbook, figuring your taxes, printing form letters and mailing labels, and so on. In order for a computer to use the software, it must be loaded into RAM (random-access memory) from ROM (read-only memory) or magnetic computer media such as cassette recording tape or disks, which we'll talk about at length a bit later in this chapter.

Not too long ago, the only way you could get software was to write it yourself. That's fine for simple tasks like balancing your checkbook, but if you want to write a program to set up a whole accounting system, it can turn into a major undertaking. At some point you'll probably want to try your hand at doing some simple programming — see Chapter 6 for the basics—but in general, you'll be buying the software you need instead of writing it yourself.

There are literally thousands of computer software packages available. These programs have been written by experts and thoroughly checked to make sure they're "bug-free." In computer jargon, a "bug" is any problem with a program that doesn't let it run correctly. The longer the program, the more the chance that major bugs will show up.

SPEAKING THE COMPUTER'S LANGUAGE

Although you don't have to know how to write a computer program to use a home computer, you do

Bugs in a computer program keep it from working properly. The software you buy has already been debugged.

have to know how to communicate with it—even if all you want to do is plug in a ready-to-use program. But communicating with a computer is easier than you think — you don't have to learn a whole new language, or use complicated math or electronics calculations. All you have to do is remember a few simple words—in English. No, computers don't *all* know English — but home computers speak a language of their own, specially designed to be easy to use and remember. Before we go on to software itself, we'll take a look at the way it's written — the language it's written in — and the way the program instructions are actually fed to the computer. This is probably the most important and least understood area concerning computers. And you'll need to know something about it so you can hold your own with a salesperson in a computer store.

Machine Language

Just as human language consists of a collection of words put in a logical order to make them understandable, a computer language is a set of operating instructions to the computer. As we discussed in Chapter 2, the microprocessor — the brains of a computer — can only understand binary numbering, the 1s and 0s — or, more basically, voltage (on) or no-voltage (off). Combinations of 1s and 0s are strung together to make each "word" telling the computer to do one simple thing like add two numbers.

The only way you could communicate with early computers was to sit punching in 1s and 0s into the machine all day. This binary numbering system is called *machine language*, because it's the only language the computer directly understands. To see how complicated and boring this method of programming a computer could be, look at a simple program to add two numbers. In machine language, it might look something like this:

```
10110110  (GET A NUMBER FROM MEMORY.)
01101101  (GET ANOTHER NUMBER FROM MEMORY.)
11110101  (ADD THE TWO NUMBERS TOGETHER.)
00110110  (PLACE THE TOTAL INTO MEMORY.)
```

As you can see, even the simplest program could take a long time to write, not to mention that there's a good chance of making a mistake. If even one of the 1s or 0s was in the wrong place, the program either wouldn't work at all or would give a wrong answer.

Assembly Language

As computers became more and more essential to businesses, the machine-language programmers just couldn't keep up with the demand. "There's got to be a better way," said the computer designers. And it didn't take long for computer experts to come up with something called *assembly language*, in which a short term took the place of those long strings of 1s and 0s. An assembly language program to add two numbers might look something like this:

```
LD B,1      (LOAD A NUMBER FROM MEMORY.)
LD A,100    (LOAD ANOTHER NUMBER FROM MEMORY.)
ADD         (ADD THE TWO NUMBERS TOGETHER.)
LD C,00F    (PLACE THE TOTAL IN A NEW MEMORY LOCATION.)
```

Another program called an assembler acted as an intermediary between the assembly language program and the computer, translating the assembly language into the same 1s and 0s the computer can understand. But as you might imagine, assembly language is still a long, involved, and error-prone process.

High-level Languages

To improve on assembly language, high-level languages were developed. They're called high-level languages because they're close to—but not quite the same as — plain English. You've probably already heard about high-level languages such as COBOL or

Home computers speak their own language, but all you need to know is a few simple words — in English. Ready-to-use software makes it easy; the program translates your instructions into the language the computer understands.

FORTRAN. COBOL, which stands for COmmon Business-Oriented Language, and FORTRAN, an acronym for FORmula TRANslation, were the first high-level languages developed for large computers. COBOL is designed mainly for business purposes, while FORTRAN is a mathematically oriented language used for scientific or engineering applications.

High-level languages, such as COBOL and FOR-

TRAN, vastly simplified the process of writing computer programs. For example, all the individual statements needed in machine or assembly language to add two numbers could be reduced to a single line:

```
TOTAL = A + B
```

Simplified versions of COBOL and FORTRAN are available for most personal computers, but as we'll see, there's a much easier way to program if you must do it yourself. It's called BASIC, and it's the language almost all home computers are programmed to understand.

Basic BASIC

The most widely used high-level computer language today is called BASIC, an acronym for Beginner's All-purpose Symbolic Instruction Code. This language was developed in 1965 at Dartmouth University, to make it as simple as possible to program computers. Because it's so easy to use, it caught on quickly. Many of the ready-made programs you can buy for a home computer are written in some form of BASIC, and almost all home computers have built-in ROM (ready-only memory) that lets them understand BASIC. Different manufacturers use slightly different *dialects* of the language, but this isn't important unless you want to do your own programming, as discussed in Chapter 6.

Although you might feel intimidated by the idea of learning how to program a computer, it's far from being an esoteric art practiced only by programmers and other computer professionals. Thanks to high-level languages like BASIC, anyone can learn how to write a simple program, in a surprisingly short period of time. Although many people never get past the baby talk stage of BASIC, you'll be surprised to see what even a simple program can do once you've typed it into your computer.

Writing a complex program is still a long and careful process — we haven't yet reached the point where we can communicate with a computer in plain English. If you're going to do your own programming, you still have to break up a task into its simplest steps, and if you misplace even one letter in a long program, the whole thing won't run.

Someday that will change — you'll be able to tell your computer, "balance the checkbook," and it will. In the meantime, there are plenty of programs that will do most of the work for you. That's why the "canned" ready-to-use programs have become so popular—to use them, you don't have to know anything about computer programming. All you have to do is use the keyboard to enter all the individual pieces of information. These programs are often called *applications programs*, because they've been written for a specific application. If you'd like to try your hand at some BASIC computer programming, you'll have an opportunity in Chapter 6.

THE OPERATING SYSTEM: A GO-BETWEEN

As far as the computer is concerned, one of the most important pieces of software it deals with is something called the *operating system*, which is built in. "The operating system" is one of the most commonly used phrases in computer jargon, but you won't have to worry much about it—either to buy a computer or to use one. The explanation that follows is all you need to hold your own with computer salesmen.

Essentially, the computer's operating system is the

go-between between the software you might buy, such as a checkbook-balancing program, and your computer. Although the program tells the computer what it needs to do, there has to be an additional piece of software that acts as a traffic cop. That's what the computer's built-in operating system does. It works with a part of the microprocessor — the "brains" — to keep all the electrical signals going about their circuit paths in an orderly manner. It also makes sure that there's space available in the computer's memory to store results, and keeps the microprocessor from trying to do more than one thing at a time.

The operating system acts as a traffic cop — it keeps the program's electrical signals moving the right way through the computer's circuits. It also keeps the computer from trying to do more than one thing at a time.

If you'll be using a floppy disk and disk drive — more about those later in this chapter—a special disk operating system (DOS), or disk controller, will be needed, too. In some cases this system, which coordinates the transfer of information to and from a floppy disk, may be built into the disk drive. But there's a possibility that it isn't, and may need to be installed in your computer's memory.

Most software is written to run with a specific operating system, but because manufacturers call their computers by brand names all you have to do is buy software that's written for that brand name. As long as the software you buy clearly says it will operate on your brand of computer — Apple, for instance, or IBM—you don't have to worry about what operating system it's for. Most software is now being labeled this way. If a software package isn't clearly marked, check with the software dealer to make sure it will run in your computer.

A few computer manufacturers make computers that can use more than one operating system. This is so their machines can run a wider variety of software. In addition, some companies offer add-on operating systems that you can buy on floppy disks and load into your computer's memory.

One operating system that you'll hear a lot about in computer stores is CP/M, which stands for Control Program for Microprocessors. CP/M has become the standard operating system for many small computers, and there are literally thousands of programs written to run with it. Depending on which computer you decide to buy, CP/M may or may not be a standard feature; if it isn't standard, it may or may not be available as an option. Most low-cost home computers can't handle CP/M, and this operating system also adds to the cost of a computer, because it requires the use of expensive floppy disk drives.

SERVICE SPECIAL

Valid for:
MR L CROOKER

Offered by:
COURTESY FORD

$ 21.00

Any Applicable Taxes Extra.

FRONT END ALIGNMENT SPECIAL.................

CHECK AND ADJUST CASTER, CAMBER AND TOE-IN. PASSENGER CARS ONLY. (VEHICLES EQUIPPED WITH MACPHERSON STRUT SUSPENSIONS INCLUDE TOE-IN ADJUSTMENT ONLY.)

EXPIRES 02-28-87   SA 174013   1FTHX25L3GKB24551

CP/M is nice to have if you can afford it, but don't worry if it isn't available—there's plenty of software around for computers that use other operating systems.

THE MANY SOFTWARE MEDIA

In the broadest sense of the term, computer software is a big part of your life whether you know it or not. Magazine subscription cards are punched with coded slots so that the information you supply can be read by a computer. It's more than likely that you've also handled other punched cards designed for computers to read—many companies use them to keep track of their employees' paychecks, and the U.S. Treasury uses them on tax refund and Social Security checks.

Another common form of computer software is the Universal Product Code, the pattern of black bars that appears on everything from canned peas and boxes of cereal to magazine covers and packages of candy. At the checkout counter, the bars are read by a light beam to tell a central computer what's being checked out. The computer instantly identifies the product, tells the cash register the item's price, and subtracts the item from its memory, giving the store manager an up-to-the-minute record of what's selling and what needs to be ordered. Most major chains that use this code system have a central computer that may be located hundreds of miles away from the store you shop in. Telephone lines are used to interconnect all stores to a single computer system.

Most of the ready-made software, or programs, that are made for your home computer are recorded on *magnetic media*. This sounds complicated, but you're probably already using one form of magnetic computer information—the dark-colored strip running across the back of most credit cards and bank money cards is a strip of magnetic recording tape that tells a computer about you and your account.

The most common forms of magnetic media used for home computers are cassette recording tape and floppy disks. Both of these forms also involve hardware, the mechanical means of feeding the software's information into the computer. Chapter 4, "Peripherals: Increasing Your Computer's Power," explains how cassette tape and floppy disks are physically used with a computer.

Cassette Tape

You're probably well-acquainted with recording tapes in cassette form. They've become the most common method of making music portable. These days, it's just about impossible to go outdoors without seeing someone, headphones on, carrying a portable stereo player. Cassette tapes are coated with an extremely thin coating of magnetic material, and the music is recorded in the form of varying voltages. The circuitry in your cassette tape recorder can also take those voltages and convert them back into music. Much the same thing is done for computer software on cassette tape.

A computer program can easily be stored on cassette recording tape. The big advantage in this type of computer program storage is cost. There's a good chance you already have a cassette tape recorder that you can plug right into a home computer. Check carefully, though; some computers require special cassette recorders, made by the same company that made the computer.

If you listen to a cassette tape that contains a computer program, you'll hear a confusing jumble of tones. That's because the program is stored in mag-

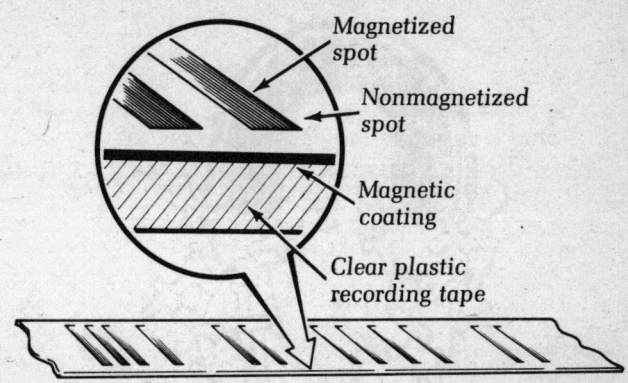

Recording tape is clear plastic tape with a magnetic coating. Magnetized spots are read as 1s, nonmagnetized spots as 0s.

netized regions on the tape as a series of voltages, which produce audio tones when the tape is played back. Because, as we've mentioned many times, the computer basically only understands 1s and 0s, the program is stored on cassette tape using two different tones: one for the 1s and one for the 0s. After the programmer writes and tests his program, he transfers the long stream of 1s and 0s to the tape with these tones.

By computer standards, the speed at which cassette tapes store and play programs is as slow as a snail. It might take more than five minutes to load a program from a tape into the computer's memory. That doesn't sound like too much time, but if you'll be using your computer often, the time you have to sit waiting for a program to load can seem like forever.

There are a couple of other disadvantages to cas-

Cassette tapes and floppy disks are both forms of magnetic media, and both can be damaged by exposure to a strong magnet.

sette tape, too. Tape has some physical problems—it can be damaged by exposure to a magnet, and leaving a tape in sunlight can destroy the programs or other data stored on it. If you use a long tape, you may have to spend quite a bit of time looking for an individual program, and that can be frustrating. In addition, much of the most popular software, including the best game programs, are not available on cassette tape—only on floppy disks.

Floppy Disks and Disk Drives

The more you hear about home computers, the more you're going to hear about floppy disks, which are sometimes called diskettes. A floppy disk is another form of magnetic medium, a circular disk of light plastic coated with magnetic material just like the type used in cassette recording tape. Information is stored, in the same 1s and 0s as with tape, in a series of concentric rings around the surface of the disk, something like a phonograph record. Each collection of information, or data, is called a *file*. It's not difficult to see why. If you think of a floppy disk as the equivalent of a file drawer — which also stores information—each collection of information is put in a file folder. It's much the same on a floppy disk, except that the information is stored as magnetic information.

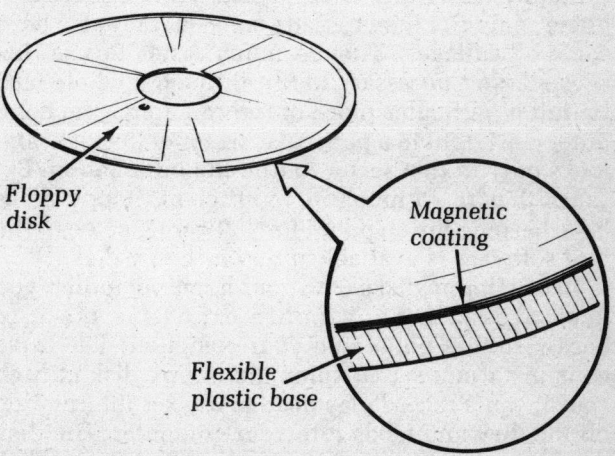

Floppy disks use the same coding system as tape; data is stored in a magnetic coating on the flexible plastic base.

A floppy disk is rather fragile, so it comes in its own plastic sleeve, or envelope, which you never remove. Holes punched in the sleeve allow the computer to get the information off the disk with a record/play head, which is similar to the head that tape recorders use. Like cassette tapes, floppy disks can be damaged by exposure to a strong magnet, or to direct sunlight.

Floppy disks come in 8-inch and 5¼-inch sizes. The smaller one, which is more generally used for home computers, is often called a minifloppy disk. These disks are called "floppy" because they are floppy if you hold them by the edge; but the name also distinguishes them from "hard" disks—expensive computer accessories often used in business. As you might imagine, hard disks have a much more solid base — normally aluminum — on which the magnetic material is coated.

Floppy disks are more expensive to use with a home computer than cassette tape, but they also have some advantages. They're much faster to use, because it isn't necessary to run through a whole tape to find a particular piece of information—the computer goes right to a particular sector of the disk, and looks only in that sector to find the information. Because they're so much more efficient, floppy disks have become the standard for software—some of the best software is available *only* on floppy disk.

To use floppy disks with your home computer, you need a disk drive, a rather expensive piece of hardware that plugs into your computer. The drive contains a motor that spins the floppy disk at high speed, and a record/play head that takes information off the disk and feeds it to your computer. The disk drive can also store new information on a floppy disk when you or the program tell the computer to do so.

Interesting enough, the information stored on a

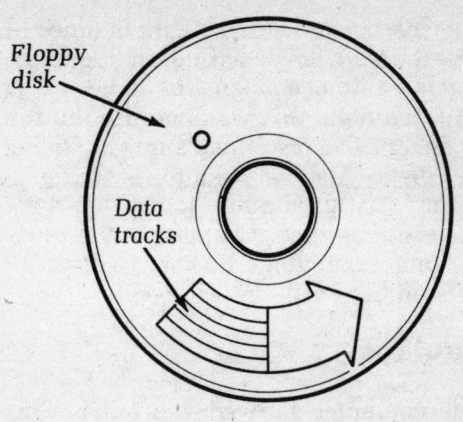

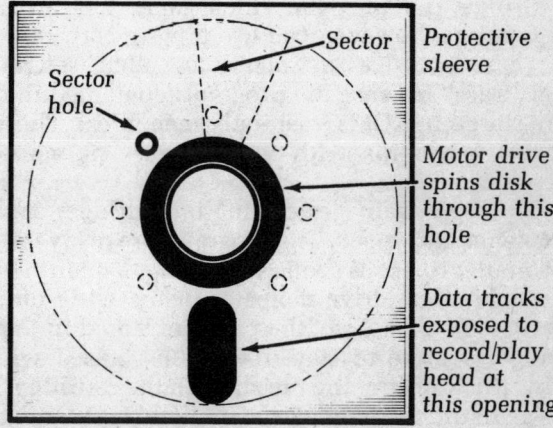

A floppy disk looks like a 45-rpm record, but it's never removed from its sleeve. Data is stored in sectors, in tracks like a record's grooves; the disk drive spins the disk and reads the information through holes in the sleeve.

floppy disk isn't contained in a series of tones like a cassette tape. Instead, the data (information) is stored in areas that have either a magnetic charge (a 1) or no charge (a 0). It's done this way because the floppy disk drive operates so fast; there's no way the computer could distinguish between tones. To the computer, a floppy that used audio tones would sound like one continuous tone. Chapter 4, "Peripherals: Increasing Your Computer's Power," will give you more details on how disk drives operate.

Plug-In Cartridges

Some home computer software is available in the form of plug-in cartridges, or modules. The most familiar examples are the plug-in game cartridges sold by many companies for home video game systems that use your TV set. All you do is plug in the cartridge and play the video game. Not all home computers, however, can use plug-in cartridges.

These cartridges are sometimes called "software in hardware" because the programs contained in them are stored in ROMs (read-only memories). These are miniature chips with the software permanently stored.

The big advantages of plug-in cartridges are convenience and speed. The programs are ready for your computer to use as soon as you plug them in. There's no noisy disk drive motor or delay while the program is loaded. Also, the program stored in the cartridge is there to stay; it can't be erased without physically destroying the chips in the cartridge. This is a distinct advantage over both tape and disk, which aren't too hard to damage or accidentally erase. If you want absolutely foolproof operations in a computer, it's worth considering a model that accepts plug-in cartridges as well as tape and floppy

Plug-in cartridges are much less vulnerable to damage than either floppy disks or cassette tapes—the programs stored in them can't be erased unless the chips inside the cartridge are physically destroyed.

disks; but remember that there isn't as much software available on cartridges as on floppy disks.

WHAT KINDS OF SOFTWARE ARE AVAILABLE?

As we mentioned at the beginning of this chapter, no matter how powerful and expensive a computer you buy and no matter how many accessories you connect to it, without software your pride and joy is like a television set tuned to a blank channel—useless. But how do you begin to choose software—tapes, disks, or cartridges—for your computer?

Listing all the software available for home computers would take a whole thick book, and because new software is being introduced every month, it would be difficult if not impossible to keep such a listing up to date. One of the best ways to learn about new software is to subscribe to one or more of the many computer magazines, where the advertisements are often as interesting as the articles. Browse through any issue, and you'll see ads for all sorts of software, some of it new and some that's been around for a while. Because of this veritable blizzard of software, most magazines have a new product section that lists newly released software. The Bibliography in this book lists some of the best computer

Many home computers are designed to work with more than one type of software; you can buy programs on disks, in cassettes, or in cartridges.

magazines. Keep these in mind as you search for the software you want.

Although it's almost impossible to list all the software available, there are several general categories that are worth considering — games, household problem-solving, education, and business are the most important.

Game Software

One of the biggest and most popular categories of home computer software is games. In fact, chances are that you might be drawn to buying a home computer because you've seen a flashy game demonstration in a local department store or computer store. Computer games can be loosely divided into two types: those that require fast thinking and reflexes and those that are more intellectually oriented. Games are becoming more and more sophisticated, and many combine fast arcade-style action and the intelligent thinking required of adventure games.

The fast-action games are often based on games that have become popular in arcades. In many cases, the computer games are as good as what you can find in your local arcade—and you don't have to put in a quarter every time you want to play. By the way, arcade games are actually small computers dedicated to the purpose of game-playing. They have a built-in microprocessor, and the actual game program is stored in ROM (read-only memory) chips.

Don't be turned off by the term "intellectually oriented" games. These computer games are as much fun as many fact-action arcade-type games, and at the same time, they make you do some careful thinking. The most common example of these games is "adventures." In an adventure, you're given a puzzle to solve, such as finding gold in a maze.

Along the way, you may run into roadblocks, monsters, and other obstacles. Your job is to figure out how to overcome the obstacles. Adventures were the first real computer games, developed by bored computer programmers to liven up their leisure hours. The first adventures were designed for use on large computer systems and were text only — no fancy pictures. Today's adventure games use the colorful graphics capabilities of home computers to their full extent, drawing very detailed pictures.

Most games for home computers are fairly expensive. Because there are so many, it's wise to try them out before buying. If you want suggestions on what games to buy, ask people who own home computers; they tend to accumulate quite a collection of games, and are a good source of advice.

Software for the Household

Software for household problem-solving is one of the fastest-growing areas for personal computers. There's a wide variety of such software available, with the list growing every day. Next to computer games, the most popular software for home use is designed to help you keep track of your finances and possessions. Today's home finance software will do a lot more than just help you balance your checkbook; it can keep a running total of income and expenditures, plan your budget, and help you with investment decisions. There are tax programs available that will keep records and even figure your taxes and fill out the tax form—when used with a printer. The more you think about it, the more you'll realize that there are all sorts of uses for a personal computer around your home. Software is available to plan menus, keep track of energy use, and tell you how long it will take to pay back your investment in extra insulation. Programs called *database managers* are also useful around the home, because they help you keep lists of your belongings for insurance purposes. If you're involved with civic groups, you can keep names and addresses in mailing lists. And when used with word processors — special software that lets you write letters and reports, most often used for business—your mailing list can be used to automatically send form letters to members of your group.

Educational Software

If you have children, a home computer can be a smart investment. More and more companies are using the two-way communication of computers to develop software designed to teach children math, reading, and a variety of related subjects. If you want to give your preschooler a jump on the other kids, you can buy a program that will teach him the basics of math and the alphabet. And programs are available that complement the teacher's efforts as your youngsters continue to grow. Most of these educational programs use fancy color graphics to emphasize their points.

There are also educational programs available for adults. Want to learn a foreign language? There's software available for that, as well as a variety of other teaching programs. The educational software area is one of the fastest-growing areas today.

Business Software

The vast majority of software developed for computers is designed for business use. That's not too surprising when you stop and think of the hundreds of thousands of computers in use, most are used in business. Over the past few years, personal com-

Educational software can give your kids a head start. There are many teaching programs, on a variety of subjects.

puters have become more and more popular in business, gradually replacing the huge machines that people still think of when they hear the term "computer." Many managers of both small and large businesses have personal computers on their desks.

Because so many personal computers are used in business, many software companies are concentrating on developing programs for business applications. It's not hard to see why. Business software often sells for several hundred dollars, although many low-cost business programs are available for much less than that.

If you're going to be using your computer mainly for entertainment and home record-keeping, you probably won't be interested in any of this business software. But if you run a business from your home or have other business-related uses for a computer, you should look into some of this software. Word processing is one type of business software that many home-computer owners find useful. Word processing gives you, essentially, a typewriter with a memory — you can move words, sentences, and paragraphs around, and add material right in the middle of something else. Some programs actually check your spelling! Word processing is a great boon for anyone who does a lot of writing; you should look into it if you're planning to write the great American novel. Once you've used word processing, it's hard to go back to using an ordinary typewriter.

If any of this sounds interesting to you, you'll find that most computer stores specialize in business software. They'll be able to give you advice. It also pays to ask for advice from other computer owners who have used the software you're interested in.

HOW TO BUY SOFTWARE

It isn't easy to walk into a store and buy software — there are literally thousands of programs available. Look through a computer magazine or walk into a computer store and you'll see what we mean. Obviously, the first consideration is whether the software you're interested in will run on your computer. This is usually easy, because a software package is always marked to tell you which computers it will work on.

It may also tell you how much memory your computer needs to use the software, and sometimes what microprocessor it works with. But all that really matters is the brand name and the memory requirement.

As you browse among the software available at a computer store, you'll probably be shocked at some of the prices on software packages. One of the first questions people ask about software is, "Why is it so expensive?" How come a software package costs $30, $100, $500, or even more? There are several reasons. Unlike a phonograph record, which is often recorded in a few days, a computer program can take hundreds, even thousands of hours to write. Getting software from an idea to a package on your dealer's shelf is a long and complicated process, and in general, the more expensive a program is, the more time and effort it took to create it. The price is high, but what you're really buying is the expert knowledge and time of the programmers — and, of course, the convenience of being able to just plug it in.

The Quality Software Library

Starting your library of computer software is a serious matter. Taking the time to carefully choose your software is as important as the time you spend deciding which computer is right for you. In fact, it won't take long for your software collection to exceed the cost of your computer hardware.

The question of software quality is a more sticky one. How do you tell whether the program you want to buy will do what it says it will? The best advice is, unfortunately, "let the buyer beware." Most software isn't returnable once you open the package. If you're considering mail-order software, the largest companies are often your best bet, as are the computer manufacturers themselves. They have a large reputation at stake.

Word of mouth is also a good indicator of what software is reliable. Go to a meeting of a computer club; there's a good chance there's one in your area—ask your local computer store dealer. A computer club often has people who are well-acquainted with all sorts of software, and they'll be happy to share their opinions on what you should buy and what you should stay away from.

When you find a software package that interests you, you'll have to make sure it will do what the manufacturer says it will do. Although most stores will replace a software package that has a defective floppy disk or cassette tape, you won't be able to return the package after you run it through your computer. In most cases, a computer store will have a demonstration copy of the software and the instruction manual that goes with it. Have the software demonstrated for you and examine the manual closely—it might not be well written, or might be too technical for you.

Sometimes, a software package will contain printed information about the manufacturer's policy regarding replacement copies of floppy disks in case your original one is damaged or wears out. But to take advantage of this you must send in a registration card that will be included in the software package. If the software package doesn't say anything about replacing disks, be sure to ask the software dealer about the company's policy before you buy.

It's a good idea to develop a close working relationship with your local computer store dealer, too. Computer dealers usually know quite a lot about software and hardware, and are willing to share their knowledge. Although any individual store can only carry only a small fraction of available computer software, a dealer will usually let you try out the software in the store before you buy it. That's the best way to make sure you'll be happy with it.

Software for Free

Believe it or not, there's an alternative to buying lots of expensive software: thousands of programs are available for next to nothing—or even free. There's a catch, though—in almost all cases, the programs are multi-page listings of BASIC programs. Because every computer manufacturer uses a slightly different form of BASIC, you may have to make some changes in the printed program, so your computer can understand it. And besides making sure that they'll run on your home computer, you may have to spend hours painstakingly typing the programs on your computer keyboard. But considering the cost of packaged software, free programs might be worth the work to you, especially if your home computer budget is limited — even if you can't find exactly what you want, and have to make changes.

Where do you find these free programs? Computer books and magazines are often full of them, and university libraries are an especially good source for such books and periodicals. Many computer clubs have a program exchange, where you're likely to find a lot of free software. You may even get your programs on floppy disk or cassette tape from a club or a user's group, for just the cost of the disk or tape. Make sure, though, that this software is in the public domain, or was developed by the person who's offering it. Just as with phonograph records or videocassette tapes of movies, it's illegal to make distribution copies of copyrighted computer software, and there can be other problems, too, as explained below.

Many libraries have a wide range of computer software in books and magazines. These programs have to be typed into your computer—but they're free. And whatever your field is, you may find just what you've been looking for.

Piracy and Copy Protection

One of the stickiest problems of the growing computer industry is piracy — the illegal copying and resale of software. Although it might seem attractive to pick up a copy of the latest computer game for $5 from someone instead of the $35 the software company may be charging for it, don't do it! Not only is it illegal, but you won't get a guarantee; you won't get service if the program doesn't work; there won't be instructions, which are often essential in order to use the software; and the copy may be bad and not work on your computer. Good commercial software is expensive, but it protects you against all these risks.

The biggest problem with software piracy is that it's stifling the development of new computer software. A number of software companies have gone out of business over the past few years because of the money they lost to pirated copies of their software. Today, many software companies are fighting back by putting "copy protection" in their software. These are sophisticated programming techniques that prevent someone from making a copy of the program. This is usually done only on floppy disks, because few expensive programs come on cassette tape.

Copy protection, however, works both ways. It's long been standard operating procedure by computer users to make a backup copy of a program as soon as they buy it, to put the original away in a safe place, and to use the copy. That way, if something happens to the copy — cassette tapes and floppy disks do get damaged and wear out—you can get out the original and make another copy. Copy protection, however, prevents you from doing this. Most companies who copy-protect their programs will sell you a low-cost backup disk when yours wears out; but that doesn't help if you ruin your tape or disk in the middle of an important project. It's a good idea to find out the manufacturer's policy on backups before you buy any software.

Pirate software is cheap, but risky—there's no guarantee, and you can't be sure these programs will work on your computer.

Chapter 4

Start with a simple computer and go on from there—with peripherals, accessories that step up the power and versatility of the basic machine. You can add a printer, a phone connection, a joystick—and much more!

Peripherals: Increasing Your Computer's Power

PERIPHERALS ARE computer accessories — hardware that increases the power and versatility of your home computer by helping you get information into and out of it as quickly and efficiently as possible. In this chapter, we'll look at various input, output, and input/output peripherals — gadgets that can greatly expand the capabilities of even the least expensive home computers. We'll also look at a peripheral that isn't just added on, but built in — extra memory.

Some of the accessories we'll discuss are similar — and in some cases identical — to the ones used with much more expensive and powerful business computers. And as you might expect, some of these peripherals are expensive. In fact, some of these extras can cost as much as — and sometimes more than — a home computer itself. But as you'll see, the additional expense can often be well worth the price.

CASSETTE TAPE RECORDERS

A few years ago, the familiar audio tape cassette was the standard method of storing and distributing software for home computers. Cassette tape recorders have one big advantage over other input/output devices — they're inexpensive. But as we discussed in Chapter 3, the disadvantages of storing computer programs and other information on cassette tape far outweigh this cost advantage.

Besides being excruciatingly slow, cassette tape recorders are unable to swap data back and forth quickly with the computer — a major problem with the sophisticated software available today. Floppy disk drives are automatic — the computer controls the movement of the disk and the drive's record/play head. Cassette tape recorders, unlike disk drives, are manually operated; you must physically start and stop the recorder and rewind or fast-forward the tape. The process of using cassette tape is a slow, error-prone, and relatively demanding one.

Except for some very inexpensive household and entertainment programs, less and less software is available on cassette tape. In fact, some personal computer makers no longer sell cassette tape recorders or even provide a place to plug them into their computers. If you do want to get started in computing with a cassette tape recorder, you can probably use a machine you already have; you may only need to buy a special plug-in cord to connect the recorder to a computer. But you should check first; some home computers require cassette tape recorders with special circuitry.

FLOPPY DISK DRIVES

Floppy disks, which look something like thin 45-rpm phonograph records protected by a plastic sleeve or envelope, have become the standard for home computer software—the most common way of entering and storing information. And to use floppy disks with a home computer, you need a floppy disk drive, a special input/output device that plugs into your computer. The drive contains two important components: a motor that spins the disk at high speed, and a record/play head that takes information off the magnetic disk and feed it to the computer. It also records new information on the disk when you —or the computer program—tell the computer to do that.

This record/play system works in much the same way as the one on a cassette tape recorder does. The main difference is that the head on the disk drive actually moves back and forth across an opening in the disk's protective sleeve as the disk spins below it; the head on a cassette tape recorder is stationary.

The information on the floppy disk is stored in the binary form the computer's microprocessor understands—the system of magnetic charge/no-charge 1s and 0s introduced earlier in this book. But to coordinate the transfer of information between the computer and disk drive, you also need a special disk operating system, or disk controller. This controller is sometimes built into the disk drive, but it may have to be added to your computer's memory. Be sure to check this out when you're looking at disk drives.

Working With a Disk Drive

There are several advantages to having a floppy disk drive for your home computer. The biggest one is that the best software is available only on floppy disks. This is because a disk holds much more information than an audio cassette tape, in a form that's much easier for the computer to get to.

Another disk-drive plus is speed. Even the longest computer program takes only seconds to load into a computer from a floppy disk, because a disk is a *random-access* device. Don't let that technical term throw you. All it means is that when you tell the computer to find a program on a disk, the record/play head goes directly to the program without having to look through all the information that comes before it. It's able to do this because every floppy disk has a *directory*, a piece of coded magnetic information that tells the computer where a particular program is lo-

A floppy disk looks like a thin 45-rmp record, protected by a plastic sleeve. It's "played" with a disk drive.

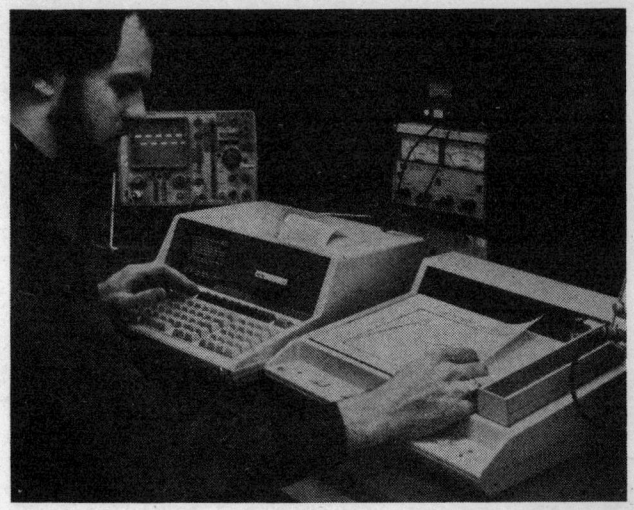

The best software requires a floppy disk drive, because it's available only in disk form. You may also want other peripherals, such as a plotter, to use with these advanced programs.

cated on the disk—it's like a book's table of contents. Once the computer finds the program, it's loaded into the computer's memory in a split second, because the floppy disk is spinning at hundreds of revolutions per minute. The faster it goes, the faster the information is picked up.

If you're confused about exactly how the computer finds information on a floppy disk, think of a long-playing phonograph record. To find the particular song you want to listen to, you look at the record label or at the list on the record jacket, find the track where the song is, and put the tone arm's needle down in that area. That's random access. The floppy disk system works the same way.

A floppy disk drive's speed and ability to random-access programs are also extremely important because many programs require the computer to continually get information from the disk and put information on the disk. That's almost impossible to do using a cassette tape — not only would it take a very long time, but the computer has no way of rewinding a tape cassette to look for a particular section of a program, unless you rewind the tape yourself.

A disk drive is by far the fastest way to get information into and out of your computer.

Floppy disks have only one real disadvantage — cost. Although the disks themselves are relatively inexpensive — about $3 to $5, depending on the brand — the disk drive you need for them can easily add $300 to $500 to the cost of your home computer system. Floppy disk drives are available for virtually all home computers. Consider carefully whether you really need one; in most cases, despite the price, you'll find that you do.

How to Choose a Disk Drive

Finding the right disk drive for your home computer isn't difficult, because you don't have a lot of choice — not every disk drive will work with every computer, for a number of technical reasons. In general, floppy disk drives are made for specific computer models. Hooking them up is a simple matter of plugging in a cable, putting a disk in the drive, and turning the machine on. Both computer manufactur-

Disk drives are made for specific computer models. This drive is equipped with a special controller.

ers and independent companies make disk drives to be used with popular brands of small computers, and the independents' disk drives are often virtually identical to the manufacturers' equipment. But your best bet is to stay with a drive made by your computer's manufacturer; this way you can be sure the drive is compatible with your computer.

A recent development is the half-thickness disk drive. As the name implies, a half-thickness drive takes up just about half the space of the standard unit. This means that you can use two disk drives in the space of one standard drive. The advantages of using more than one disk drive are discussed later in this section.

Types of Disk Drives. The 5¼-inch minifloppy disk is the standard size for home computers. There are other sizes of disks, and disk drives made to be used with them, but you'll probably never see them. Many business computers have drives made for 8-inch disks, which can store more than twice the information of the 5¼-inch disk. But these larger disks and disk drives are not available for most home computers, and almost the only programs available on 8-inch disks are for business use.

You'll also hear terms like *double-density* and *double-side* in regard to floppy disk drives. These are special types of disks and disk drives, made to increase the amount of information that can be stored on and retrieved from a disk.

Double-density drives hold twice the information on a floppy disk that ordinary drives—also referred to as *single-density* — can. This is possible because the magnetic areas that contain the computer information on the disk are packed together more tightly. Reading this information requires special disk-drive circuitry, and record/play heads that are more expensive than those used in single-density drives.

Double-side floppy disk drives use a second record/play head and additional circuitry to store and retrieve data from both sides of the disk; this also effectively doubles the information storage space. And double-density, double-side disk drives use both of these methods, and hold four times the amount of data of a single-density disk drive. For this reason, you'll sometimes hear double-density, double-side disk drives referred to as *quad-density* drives.

Double-density disk drives use a special disk with a higher-quality magnetic coating to faithfully record the tightly packed pattern of magnetic charges, and these special disks are slightly more expensive. Double-density, double-side, and quad-density disk drives aren't available for all home computers, and because they have more parts — moving and electrical — they're usually more prone to problems than standard single-density disk drives. Single-density disks and disk drives are still the most common for home computers, but this may not be the case for long. Although the more sophisticated drives are more expensive — a quad-density disk drive can cost more than $1,000 — their data capacity is so far superior that they're moving up fast in the market.

How Much Data? The amount of information a floppy disk holds is measured in "K," just like a home computer's internal memory. Each K is 1,024 bytes. Remember, there are 8 bits — individual areas of magnetic charge or no charge, 1 or 0 — in each byte. You'd think that every single-density floppy disk drive would hold the same amount of data, but this isn't the case.

The exact amount of information a floppy disk holds depends on the circuitry in the disk drive itself. A 5¼-inch single-density disk usually holds between 100K and 175K of data—the equivalent of 25 to 40 typewritten pages. Double that amount for double-density or double-side disks, and quadruple it for quad-density disks. Some 8-inch disks hold up to 750K of data.

The kind of disks—and disk drive—you should buy depends on your needs. As far as commercial software is concerned, the vast majority is available on single-density floppy disks, so a standard single-density disk drive is all you need.

How Many Drives? Although all you need to run floppy disk software is one disk drive, you may want to consider buying a second drive. "Dual floppies" come in handy if you're going to do any extensive work with your computer. Why? For example, a single floppy disk may not have enough room to hold all the data you need for a large mailing list. You could change disks, but that can be time-consuming. In addition, many advanced programs, especially for business use, need to be able to get to the information on more than one disk at the same time.

A second floppy disk drive also makes the "housekeeping" chores of copying data from one disk to another much easier—for example, making a backup disk for a new program. Copying a disk can be time-consuming with only a single disk drive. The computer has to take a part of the information on the disk, store it internally in its RAM memory, wait for you to change to a blank disk, take the information from RAM, put it on the disk, wait for you to put the original disk back in the drive, and the whole process starts again. If your original disk is full of data, you might have to change the disks 15 or 20 times! With a second disk drive, you put the original disk in one and a blank disk in the other, and simply tell the computer to copy the disk.

A second disk drive usually costs about $100 less than the first one. The reason for this is that the second machine doesn't need a controller, a special circuit board—usually built into the case holding the disk drive—that controls the transfer of data from disk to computer and back. With a pair of disk drives, or even more, only one controller is needed.

More than two disk drives can be used with a home computer—if it's necessary, you can add up to four disk drives to your computer. But for most home computer owners, two drives are ample. Four drives are needed only for advanced business applications.

The Essential Accessory. If you buy a floppy disk drive for your home computer, there's an inexpensive accessory that's absolutely necessary—a head-cleaning kit. The magnetic coating on floppy disks tends to wear out over time, just like ordinary recording tape. That's why you should make backup copies of important floppy disks if you can. As disks wear out, a residue gums up the disk drive's record/play head and makes it produce errors in reading the data on the disk. This can be a major problem, because even one misread 1 or 0 in the hundreds of thousands in a computer program can cause the entire program to run incorrectly or not at all.

A disk drive head-cleaning kit costs about $15 to $20. It consists of a special floppy disk with an absorbent pad in place of the magnetic surface. You pour a special cleaning solution (provided with the kit) on the pad and run the disk in the disk drive. The special disk cleans the residue off the drive's head. Cleaning also results in longer life for disks.

Hard Disk Drives

Although you'll probably never use them, you'll hear a lot about "hard" disks. Often called Winchesters,

Keeping the drive clean is essential, because dirt can cause errors—your program may not work at all.

hard disks are rigid disks made of aluminum and coated with the same type of magnetic material used on floppy disks. Hard disks spin at thousands of revolutions per minute, and use special disk drive heads that move over the surface of the disk at distances closer than the diameter of a dust speck.

Because of this speed and special electronic circuitry, hard disks store huge amounts of data—five to ten *million* bytes. To put that in some perspective, that's equal to well over a thousand typewritten pages, compared to the standard floppy's capacity of 25 to 40 pages. Unlike floppy disk drives, you can't change the disk in a hard disk drive. The disks are sealed in a special enclosure with filtered air, because a dust or smoke particle can cause major problems.

Hard disks are tailor-made for serious business applications, where huge amounts of data have to be available for immediate use. But they aren't normally used for home computers. Hard disk drives are far from cheap; they cost anywhere from $1,200 to $3,000. But as with many computer hardware items, their prices are declining, and may fall below $1,000 in the near future. Eventually, hard disks may become practical for use with home computers.

PRINTERS

One of the most important output devices for your home computer is a printer. If you start out without a printer, you'll find that you can save information off the video display screen by using a cassette tape or floppy disk—if you have a disk drive. But you still have to load the data back into the computer to read it off the video screen. You could take photographs of your video screen, but that's an even worse solution. If you want to record the information in a manner that's portable — that anyone can read without having to have a computer—you'll need *hard copy*, a printed document. For this reason, it won't take you long to find out that a printer is so important that it's nearly a necessity. In fact, a printer may eventually be built into most home computers.

You might consider a printer to be a one-way typewriter. This computer-controlled machine

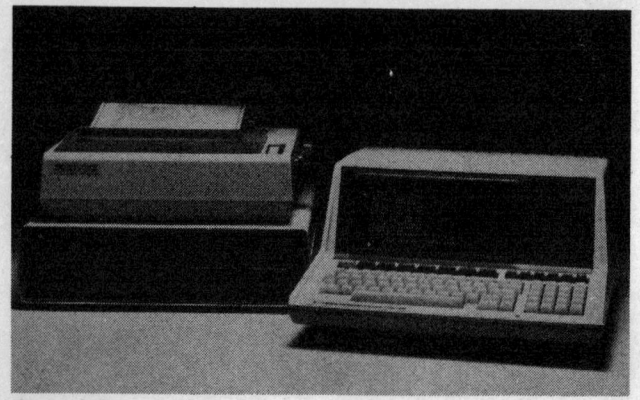

One of the most important peripherals is the printer, designed to give you a permanent, portable hard copy of your information. Especially for business uses, a printer can be nearly a necessity.

prints information that the computer feeds it, but has no provision for entering information into the computer — that's the job of the keyboard. The printer simply takes the binary code the computer uses and translates output, or data, into letters of the alphabet, numbers, or punctuation marks. Printers are tailor-made for producing hard copy, and they do it fast, efficiently, and with absolute accuracy.

If you want a printer to use with your personal computer, you'll find a wide variety available, from prices as low as $150 to as much as $2,000 and more. You'll also find that the quality and features of printers differ considerably. Take the time to learn something about the different types of printers, and don't be scared off by the jargon. Essentially, it all boils down to the way the printer forms characters on paper—*impact printers* use a *printhead* that strikes a ribbon against paper; *nonimpact printers* use special mechanisms that don't strike the paper. Once you know this basic difference, the rest is easy to follow.

Impact Printers

Impact printers can be divided into two types. One produces fully formed characters on paper in a single operation. The other forms characters from patterns of individual dots that are printed in groups. Let's look at both.

Fully Formed Character Printers: Daisy Wheels and Thimbles. Impact printers that produce fully formed characters work in the familiar way a typewriter does. A hammer strokes a movable wheel or cylinder covered with embossed characters and

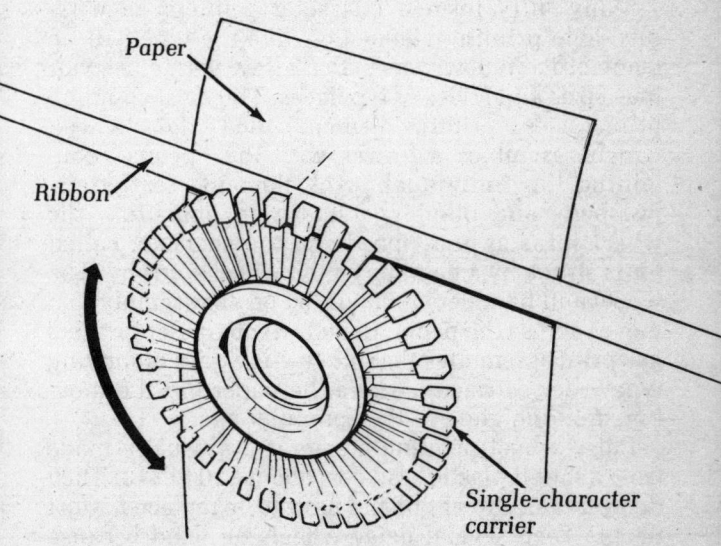

The most common kind of printer uses a printing element called a daisy wheel, with characters on the "petals."

forces the character against a carbon or inked ribbon, which strikes the paper. Manufacturers like to call printers that produce fully formed characters *letter-quality printers*. That's because the aim is to make the characters look as if they were typed by an ordinary office typewriter.

Interestingly enough, you won't find many printers that work the way old-fashioned typewriters do, with a movable arm for each character. The reason for this is speed. Printers for computers print much faster than even the fastest human typists can work. Computer printers are designed so that the print element moves as little as possible; the shorter the distance it moves, the faster the printer prints. Fully formed character printers commonly print at speeds of 40 to 55 characters a second.

Many fully formed character printers have replaceable printing elements — like the type ball on many office typewriters — that allow you to use various sizes and styles of typefaces. The most common printer uses a printing element called a *daisy wheel*, which resembles a flower with the "petals" containing the individual print elements for letters, numbers, and other characters. In operation, the wheel spins at high speed and the character called for is struck by a hammer as the wheel spins by. The wheel and hammer are mounted on an assembly that moves across the paper. In fact, all computer printers use print assemblies that move—the days of moving typewriter carriages, where the paper did the moving, are long gone in the computer age.

Daisy wheel printing elements are usually made from a tough plastic, and cost about $10 to $15. They do eventually wear out and have to be replaced. Most people keep several daisy wheels on hand because it's so easy to change type size from pica to elite, or change to a different typeface. Metal daisy wheel elements are available, too, but they can't be used with all printers, and they're much more expensive —about $40 to $50. Unless you'll be using a daisy wheel in a business where the printer must work all day, every day, a plastic daisy wheel is all you need.

There's another kind of printing element for fully formed character printers. This element, which resembles a giant thimble, looks like a daisy wheel with the spokes bent upward to form a cup. These printing thimbles are made from nylon-reinforced fiberglass and cost about $15. Just as with daisy wheels, a wide variety of different type styles is available for thimble elements.

Daisy wheel and thimble printers for home computers aren't cheap—the least expensive are almost $1,000, with prices going well beyond $3,000. But

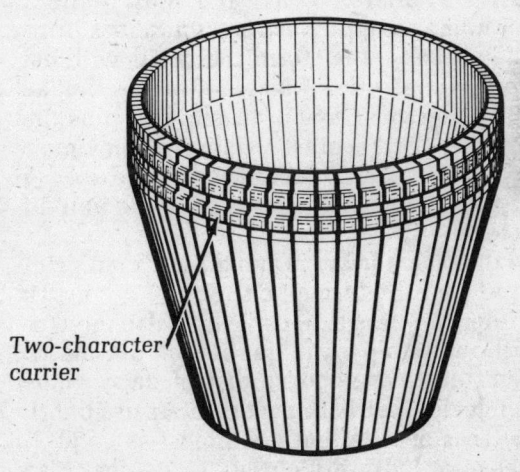

Two-character carrier

Another kind of printing element is the thimble, which looks like a daisy wheel with the spokes bent up.

these peripherals have by far the highest print quality. Do you need one? It depends on what you'll be doing with your computer and printer. Daisy wheel and thimble printers are useful if you'll be using your personal computer for extensive word processing, especially for a small business. They give a very professional appearance to letters.

Both daisy wheel and thimble printers are slow by computer standards. Even though their 10 to 50 characters per second is fast compared to even the fastest human typist, it's much slower than the up to 300 characters per second that dot-matrix printers can achieve. But speed is relative. If you'll only be printing a few letters at a time, slow printers are fine. But if you're running a business where invoices have to be sent out or long reports generated, you may need the extra speed of another type of printer.

Dot-Matrix Printers. By far the most popular printers for home computer use are *dot-matrix printers*, so called because they form characters with patterns of individual dots. Most dot-matrix impact printers have a vertical row of needle-like pins that are individually fired against a ribbon as they move across the paper. Each pin produces a single dot as it strikes the paper, and the patterns form the individual characters.

Because they have fewer moving parts than printers that produce fully formed characters, dot-matrix impact printers are less expensive and also more reliable. Although the print quality of dot-matrix printers isn't quite as good as that of daisy wheel printers, some dot-matrix impact printers use tightly packed patterns of dots that are almost as good. In fact, you have to look very closely to see that it's a dot matrix. But these special printers, because they use more moving parts, are also more expensive.

Dot-matrix impact printers are also much faster

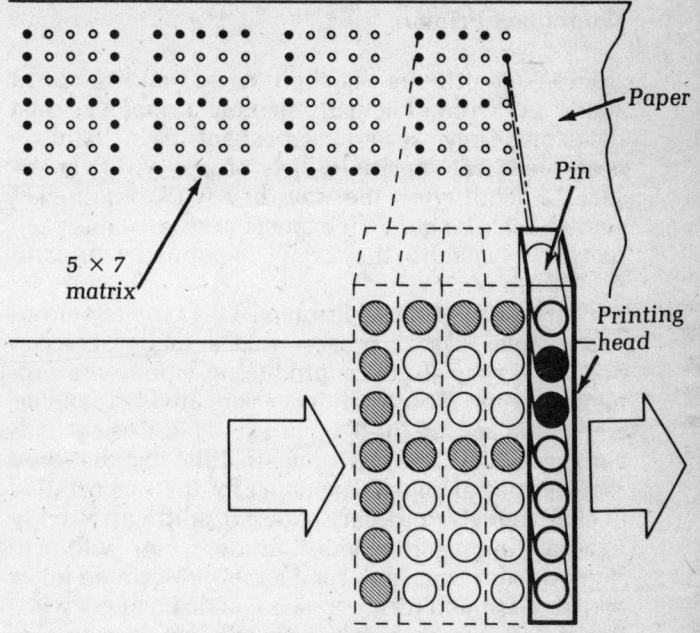

Dot-matrix printers form characters by making individual dots on the paper. The printing head has a vertical row of pins, which are fired against a ribbon as the head moves across the paper.

than fully formed character printers—speeds of 80 to 200 characters per second are common, and research is now being done that will enable these printers to produce an entire page in less than five seconds. And a good-quality dot-matrix impact printer can be bought for less than $300—an important consideration. Recently, prices of dot-matrix printers have been declining rapidly.

Nonimpact Printers

Nonimpact printers, as their name implies, print characters without actually striking a ribbon against the paper. They use various mechanisms to do this—heat, electrical sensitivity, jets of ink, and even lasers. Depending on the way they work, nonimpact printers can be either inexpensive or extremely expensive. Generally, they aren't as popular as the impact printers.

Thermal Dot-Matrix Printers. This type of nonimpact printer uses a process that actually scorches dots on a special paper, producing letters in a dot-matrix format. These printers are relatively inexpensive, often selling for $200 to $300, but this cost advantage has to be weighed against the fact that they require special paper. The paper for thermal printers doesn't look like ordinary paper; it's difficult to copy in a copying machine and it tends to fade with age. You probably wouldn't send a thermal-printed letter to a friend, much less someone you do business with. But if you need a quick copy of a program you've been working on or a short-term printout of your check this month, a thermal printer may be suitable.

Electrographic Dot-Matrix Printers. This kind of nonimpact printer combines the dot format of the dot-matrix printer with a special electrically sensitive paper, composed of a very thin aluminum foil over black paper. Needle-thin wires in the device's printhead are used to touch the paper, and an electrical current is applied. As the current flows through the wires, holes are made in the aluminum, exposing the black paper underneath. The letters formed in this way are similar to those formed by the dot-matrix impact printer.

Electrographic printers are very quiet, and about as inexpensive as thermal printers. But the special

Some printers can produce charts, graphs, and other images off the computer's video display screen.

paper they require is both expensive and difficult to store, and the printed copy is not of a high enough quality to use for business applications.

Ink-jet Printers. These nonimpact printers are just what they sound like; they actually fire a tiny jet of special ink at the paper, forming characters made up of individual dots. The ink is controlled by a magnetic field. Ink-jet printers are extremely quiet, phenomenally fast — they can print an entire page in a second — and extremely expensive, currently more than $10,000. We mention them because their price is expected to drop drastically in the next few years, perhaps to less than $1,000. Even at that price, they'll still be mainly for serious business applications.

Laser Printers. The laser, that powerful beam of light so beloved of science-fiction writers, has become a workhorse in many industries. Printers have been developed that actually scorch images on ordinary paper using a tightly focused laser beam. Right now they're as expensive as ink-jet printers, but their price will certainly fall in the years ahead.

Choosing a Printer

Just like deciding which computer is right for you, choosing a printer should be a careful process. There are quite a few factors to consider — reliability, print quality, paper cost, and service availability are just a few. Here are some of the factors you should keep in mind when you're looking at printers.

The Ribbon. All impact printers use ribbons. Is the ribbon for the printer you're considering readily available? How expensive is it? More important, how long will it last? What about changing the ribbon? Is it in a pop-in/pop-out cartridge or is changing it a messy and time-consuming job? Remember, the quality and condition of the ribbon controls the quality and legibility of the typed page. Some companies offer low-cost reusable nylon ribbons as well as one-time-use carbon ribbons that produce a crisper character image. This way, you have a choice of print quality — you can use carbon ribbon when the page has to look good, and reusable nylon ribbon when print quality isn't so important.

The Paper Feed Mechanism. There are two common methods of feeding paper through a printer. The first, called *friction feed*, is just like the roller on a standard typewriter. The method is fine for short letters, but for long, multi-page documents you'll have to sit in front of the printer and keep feeding paper by hand.

A more common approach for computer printers, especially the more expensive varieties, is *pin feed*— sometimes called *tractor feed*, because the pins pull the paper through the way a tractor pulls a plow. This method uses special continuous sheets of paper with horizontal perforations every 11 inches and holes along each side — the classic computer printout sheets you're already familiar with. A pair of plastic or metal wheels encircled by stubby pins turns and actually pulls the paper through the printer. Most computer paper is also perforated along the edges, so that you can remove the holes from the pages.

Pin-feed mechanisms add cost to a printer, because they have a number of moving parts. But if you need to print business forms or mailing labels, a pin-feed printer is a necessity. This method will keep the labels and forms lined up so that information is printed in the correct place on the paper each time. The paper used for pin-feed printers is called *fan-fold*, because it's folded like an accordian bellows every 11 inches — the length of a standard letter-size sheet of paper. Fan-fold paper costs about the same as regular paper on a per-sheet basis. It does, however, have a few disadvantages: really top-quality letter paper isn't available, and there's the chore of manually separating the sheets and tearing off the edges. Although there are machines that do that, they're too expensive for home use or even small businesses.

Printing Speed. As we mentioned, a printer's speed is specified in characters per second (cps). Fully formed character printers have speeds ranging from about 10 to 50 cps—the slowest will take more than two minutes to print a page, while the fastest will print two pages a minute. Dot-matrix printers start at about 55 cps and go up to 300 cps. At that speed, a whole page is printed in a little over 5 seconds.

But do you need such high speed? Probably not, unless you're using your computer all day, every day, and printing hundreds of bills or mailing labels. Unless speed is a major consideration, the extra convenience of a high-speed printer probably isn't worth the extra money.

Characters Per Line. Many of the lowest-cost printers will only print a 40-character line—a standard typewriter can print about 80 characters per line. Just 40 characters per line isn't sufficient for most applications, especially word processing; and this short line is useless for business applications. Many printers come with either an 80-character line or a 132-character line. For most uses, all you'll need is 80 characters. If you want to use the printer for business, though, consider one that gives you a 132-character line. It's not that much more expensive, and it's invaluable for reports and other business documents.

Type Style. There's a large variety of type styles available with fully formed character printers. All you do is pop the daisy wheel or thimble in and out for an instant change from pica to elite, or whatever style you like.

Dot-matrix printers use software control to generate a variety of type styles. Depending on the model, you can get several type styles from one printer, ranging from plain block lettering to script.

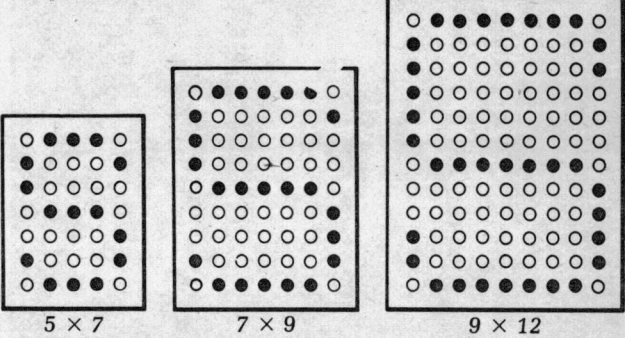

5 × 7   7 × 9   9 × 12

Not all dot-matrix printers give you the same print quality. Some printers use more dots, and produce crisper and more readable characters. Common matrix sizes are 5 rows by 7 columns, 7 by 9, and 9 by 12.

Dot-matrix printers also have the ability to print **bold** or *italic* words in the middle of a sentence without changing any equipment.

Whatever type of printer you want, be sure to take a look at a sample printout before making your purchase—that way, you won't get any surprises. Some dot-matrix printers, for example, use more dots for a crisper and cleaner image; common matrix sizes are 5 rows by 7 columns, 7 by 9, and 9 by 12. Don't buy any type of printer until you're sure the print quality will suit you.

Graphics. Some dot-matrix printers have the ability to print charts, graphs, and other graphic images off your video display screen. If this capability is available, it's probably worth getting; it's usually a relatively inexpensive option.

Interface. You should be aware that you'll have to be able to plug your printer into your computer in order for the data to get into printed form. To do this, you'll need an *interface*, an electrical gadget for

The most sophisticated dot-matrix printers can produce amazingly detailed images. If this capability is available, it's probably worth getting; it may not add significantly to the printer's price.

transferring this data. Some printers use a *serial interface*; some use a *parallel interface*; some use both. We won't go into the technical specifications, but your printer must match your computer. Talk to the computer dealer when you shop to make sure you get the proper interface for your computer.

Other Considerations. There are a few other things to consider, too. How noisy is the printer? Does it vibrate a lot? Does it buzz or beep when it runs out of paper? If it doesn't, you might lose valuable information.

Some printers have a special test feature that, at

the touch of a button, prints all the printer's characters. Some printers can even print characters upside-down or sideways. Ask for a complete demonstration before you buy.

Printer accessories are also available. These include sound-absorbing covers, special tables, and so on. They add to the convenience of a printer, but are often expensive. One excellent investment, however, is a dust cover. At $10 to $15, it will keep problem-causing dust out of your printer's delicate mechanism.

Finally, be sure the printer comes with a warranty. Because printers have many moving parts, they're more prone to problems than other computer hardware. The usual warranty period is 90 days, but some printers have a one-year warranty.

Printer Prices

Printers for personal computers can be put into three general price ranges: low (under $500); medium ($500 to $1,000); and high (over $1,000).

Many impact and nonimpact dot-matrix printers are available for under $500, including the thermal and electrographic models. They're all suitable for producing hard copies of programs, and many do an acceptable job on minor word-processing chores.

Printers in the $500 to $1,000 range make up the most popular group. They include fast dot-matrix and some of the slower fully formed character printers.

Printers that cost more than $1,000 offer impressive print quality and speed, but they're too expensive for most home computer users. Unless you'll be using your computer for something that requires the very best in hard copy, you're probably better off with a less expensive printer.

Just as personal computer technology is progressing at a rapid rate, printers, too, are evolving. Many of today's medium-cost units actually have their own built-in microprocessor that controls the printing

Joysticks, the airplane-control devices that are so much fun in video games, can be used with your computer.

process. Prices are falling rapidly. Look at the latest models before you buy. It won't be long before the features available today for more than $1,000 will cost less than $500.

JOYSTICKS

Many of the fast-action video games in arcades are played by moving the handle of a lever—a joystick—to change the position of an object on the video display screen. This input device for a home computer is like a smaller version of an airplane control stick, and is normally mounted in a small box that you hold in the palm of your hand. The box often has a button that's used for firing missiles or releasing bombs during the game. Joysticks cost about $20 to $25 a pair.

Most home computers have a place to plug in a cable for the operation of a joystick. Some games, especially for two players, require two joysticks. By the way, you can play most computer games without a joystick; many games give you the option of using certain patterns of keys. But using the computer's keyboard isn't as fast, as realistic, or as fun as using joysticks. A similar input device, called a *paddle controller*, is also available.

MODEMS

A *modem* (short for modulator/demodulator) is an input/output device that lets you link your home computer with other computers using a telephone line. This truly puts the world at your fingertips, because you can use the many computer information utilities, or services, to get news, weather, airline schedules, and other information—and you can even exchange messages via "electronic mail," with other

With a modem, you can link your computer to others, and use your phone to get a wealth of information.

home computer users anywhere in the world.

Modems convert the binary data (the 1s and 0s) the computer puts out into tones that are sent over the telephone line. At the other end of the line, another modem converts the tones back into binary code so the other computer can understand the transmission.

There are two types of modems: *acoustic couplers* and *direct-connect modems*. An acoustic coupler is a small box with rubber cups to receive your telephone's handset; you dial the number and place the handset into these cups, and your computer can "talk" to another computer. Direct-connect modems hook between your telephone and the telephone's wall jack. You still have to use your phone to dial the number, but after you're connected, you flip a switch on the modem and hang up the phone's handset. Because they don't use the low-quality microphone that most telephone handsets have, direct-connect modems are less prone to errors and more convenient to use.

Modems range in price from about $100 to more than $250. The lower-cost models are acoustic couplers; direct-connect modems are more expensive because they require more circuitry. The most expensive modems are models that transmit and receive information at higher speeds; some even automatically dial the telephone number when you enter it into your computer. A modem may eventually be built into most home computers.

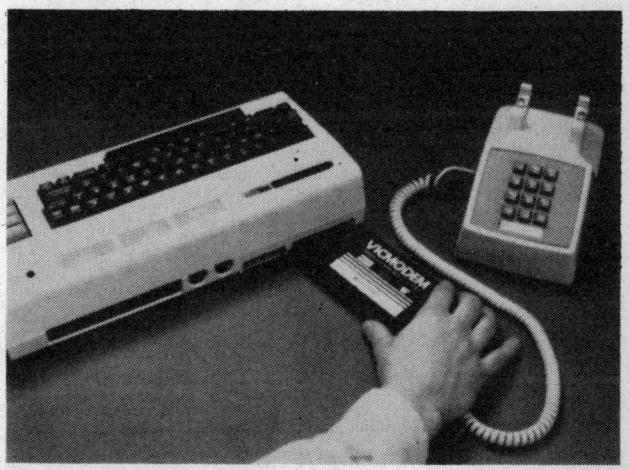

Some modems are made in the form of cartridges, and plug right into your computer. Some even dial for you!

TERMINALS

A modem lets you send and receive information over a telephone line. But it's important to note that because you're using the power of the large computers you're hooked up to, you don't need to use all the powerful computational and memory abilities of your home computer. In fact, the special software used with modems effectively disconnects many of your computer's internal features. If you feel your main interest is using computer information services, you could buy a sort of stripped-down computer designed for that purpose. This input/output device is called a *terminal*.

A terminal essentially consists of a keyboard and a video display. There are two kinds of terminals. A so-called *dumb terminal* just has the minimum circuitry you need to type in information and see the results on a video display. An intelligent or *smart terminal* has a built-in memory. Some smart terminals have one or more self-contained microprocessors, and can do many things a small computer does. In fact, though some such machines are called terminals, they're actually smart enough to be considered computers.

A terminal lets you hook up to any large computer through a telephone line. Some terminals are designed to be used with modems; some models even have a modem built into them so that all you have to do is plug the terminal into the telephone line.

Terminals come in a variety of sizes, ranging from small handheld units — designed to help traveling salesmen call in their orders from pay telephones — to large and *very* expensive models that rival home computers. The most costly terminals are designed to take the place of the keyboard and video display screen in high-priced computer systems, and they

Dumb terminals are just a keyboard and a display. Smart terminals have a built-in memory, and actually compute.

are often used to let several people use the system at the same time. This process is called time-sharing, and requires some pretty sophisticated software. Although time-sharing is mainly designed for large

Some terminals are made to work with computer information services. They may include a modem and even a printer.

computer systems, some of the more expensive personal computer systems—$5,000 to $10,000—come in the form of boxes containing the microprocessor, the memory, and other needed circuitry. If you get to the point where you want to buy one of these units, you can also choose a terminal to go along with it.

Several major manufacturers make low-priced terminals, selling for $300 to $500. These are designed to be hooked up to computer information services—a real alternative to the full-scale home computer. Besides the keyboard and sometimes a video display, these terminals often have a place to plug in a printer so that you can get a hard copy of what's appearing on the screen.

The main advantages of terminals are their

simplicity and the fact that they usually cost less than a home computer system. But you should consider getting one only if you're sure all you're going to want to do is get information over the telephone. A home computer is an immensely more powerful tool.

LIGHT PENS

An unusual input peripheral is a *light pen*. It looks very much like a ballpoint pen, with a cable coming out of one end. The cable is connected to the computer. Light pens range in price from $25 to about $125.

A light pen lets you talk to the computer without typing— all you do is point to the video display screen.

The tip of the light pen has a tiny sensor that detects light areas on the video display screen. Text and graphics produced on a video display screen are produced in exactly the same way as an ordinary television picture; a beam of electrons is swept across the screen, causing areas of the screen to light up. Because this beam is precisely controlled and repeatable, it's possible for the computer to determine exactly where the tip of the pen is pointing.

Although a light pen is a peripheral — a piece of hardware — it requires special software so the computer can work with it. Using a light pen with this software, it's possible to program a computer so that instead of having to type in your commands on a keyboard, all you do is point the pen toward a word or phrase you want the computer to act on.

PLOTTERS

A plotter is a very special kind of printer—an output device that allows a computer to draw diagrams, designs, pictures, patterns, and symbols with a ballpoint pen or felt-tip marker on paper. Plotters can even print perfectly formed numbers, letters, and punctuation marks.

Plotters were once very expensive, and they're still not too cheap. Now you can buy a plotter that can draw with as many as six colors, for less than $2,000. If you need its graphic capabilities for business purposes, the plotter can be a very useful peripheral.

POWER PROTECTORS

Most peripherals do a specific job, but there are two peripherals that exist to keep your computer working at all its tasks. One is the *line filter*—an inexpensive device, priced at about $15, that protects your

A plotter is a special kind of printer — instead of making characters like a typewriter, it draws on the paper with pens or markers. Some plotters can draw with as many as six colors.

computer from voltage surges and interference caused by appliance motors. This is important because an abrupt change in voltage can actually damage your computer hardware. The line filter will protect your computer against this kind of damage — for the price, it's a form of insurance that's well worth considering.

The second power-protector is called an *uninterruptable power supply*, or UPS. This device is a failsafe — it supplies power to your computer when your home power supply fails, long enough for you to save the volatile data stored in the computer's RAM memory. Without a UPS, you lose all the data you're working on if the power fails or the machine is accidentally unplugged while you're using the computer. Until recently, the least expensive UPS cost more than $2,000, but these devices are now available for $400 or less; as prices decline further, you may want to consider investing in a UPS. Manufacturers may also start building this protection into their computers in the future.

BRAIN POWER: ADDING MEMORY TO YOUR COMPUTER

So far, we've talked mostly about add-ons — peripherals you can use with your computer to do specific tasks. There's one other important kind of peripheral, and that's not an add-on but an add-in: extra memory, giving your computer more brain power.

Although the price of computer memory — RAM, the random-access read/write memory your computer uses to store information — is rapidly going down, many low-cost home computers come with just a minimal amount of memory: 1K, 2K, 3K, or 8K. In general, the more RAM your computer has, the more software you can run, because more sophisticated programs take up more memory space. It's best to buy a computer that has enough to meet your needs, but depending on the computer, you can usually add more memory — in a variety of ways.

Probably the minimum memory you should have is 16K — 16,384 individual locations for your computer to store information. If your computer doesn't have this capacity, you can sometimes plug in additional memory by using cartridges much like those used for home video games. Although that's a convenient and quick way to do it, all those boxes and cartridges sticking out can get in the way.

Many companies will install additional memory for you, but that requires either bringing your computer to a computer store or sending it back to the manufacturer. This is because the process requires installing memory chips in a new circuit board and wiring it into everything else. Some companies also sell plug-in memory boards for certain computers. The Apple, for instance, has special slots for these plug-in boards; all you do is open the machine's cover and plug the memory board in. Only a few home computers are built to work this way, though —and opening the cover of a computer usually voids your warranty.

What does this kind of memory expansion cost? There's no easy answer. Memory prices are falling all the time. For a 12K RAM expansion (from 4K to 16K), you can expect to pay anything from $50 to $200. Unfortunately, you can't shop around; the price depends on the specific computer you own. Prices vary from manufacturer to manufacturer, and the only reliable way to add memory is to go back to the maker of your computer. You might be tempted to get around the installation costs of additional memory by buying the chips advertised in many computer magazines, but don't do it — installing memory circuitry requires a great deal of electronics knowledge; you'll probably void the computer's warranty at the same time; and bargain chips might not work at all. Your best bet is to stick with the computer manufacturer's product for this peripheral.

Chapter 5

There are lots of computers on the market, in all shapes and sizes. Which one is right for you? Check out all the models and makers — we'll help you make sure that you and your home computer are a perfect match.

Choosing Your Home Computer

YOU'RE HOOKED! You've studied the advantages and taken a look at your checkbook balance, and you've decided to buy a home computer. Obviously, the first question on your mind is, "Which one should I buy?"

As we've stressed throughout, there are many alternatives, in both hardware and software. Before you can decide which of these alternatives is right for you, you have to answer two basic questions: "What do I want to do with it?" and "How much computer power do I need?"

Fortunately, buying a home computer system is a lot like buying quality camera or stereo equipment. You can start small, with a basic unit, and add software and peripherals as new requirements arise and your finances permit. Keep in mind that accessories and software sold by one computer company probably won't operate with a computer sold by another company. If you may want to expand your system in the future, you should buy a computer for which a lot of peripherals—and a lot of software—are available. You'll be pretty safe if you stick with the major brands, which we'll discuss later on in this chapter.

Ideally, you should buy a computer for which accessories are also available from other companies. This helps keep prices down and quality up, and assures you of a good selection. Once again, sticking with the major brands means that there will be enough accessories around.

It's usually a good bet to buy only as much computing power and accessories as you really need at first, especially because prices on such peripherals as printers and floppy disk drives are expected to decline in the next few years. But there's another side to this coin, too: many times you can get a better deal by buying a complete package from your dealer. Package arrangements include a variety of options, accessories, and software in addition to your home computer.

Complicating the choice of which computer is right for you is the fact that the home computer market is one of the fastest-growing and changing areas of consumer electronics. New computers, new peripherals, and new software are appearing on the market all the time. In this chapter, we'll take a look at a few representative personal computer lines. By knowing about the capabilities and features of these computers, you'll be better prepared to compare features if and when you decide to buy your own home computer.

The way you'll use your home computer determines the basic capabilities and the peripherals you'll need.

WHAT DO YOU WANT IT TO DO?

The question of what you want to do with your computer is the first and most important consideration when you shop. The answer to that question will narrow down your choices considerably.

Start at the low end of the price range. If you'll only want to use your computer at home for games, education, some home finance, and maybe a bit of BASIC programming, look into the smaller, less expensive machines. They're true computers, with a great deal of software available. They don't, of course, have a large memory, a full typewriter keyboard, or the ability to expand with lots of peripherals and accessories. But for basic uses, they're fine.

Although low-priced computers are fine training machines for beginners, it doesn't take long for most people to realize just what a handy machine a home computer can be. Chances are that it won't be long before you'll be using your computer for word processing, sophisticated home financial planning, and other things like handling club lists and newsletters. If you think there's the remotest possibility that you'll be getting into these areas, buy a computer that has expansion ability. You don't have to spend a great deal at first, but the ability to expand your home computer system when you want to is invaluable.

Are you going to be using your computer a great deal? If so, you'll want to consider the more sophisticated computers designed for day-in, day-out use. Besides full typewriter keyboards, they often use video displays that are designed to reduce eyestrain —an important consideration if you'll be using them all day.

FACTORS TO CONSIDER

Despite the differences in cost and appearance, all home computers do basically the same thing in the same way. What matters is efficiency, quality of construction, and—of course—the ability to do the work you want done. Once you've decided what size you want—desktop or handheld—there are several basic factors to consider in choosing your computer. We've compiled the following questions to give you an idea of what to look for. It's important to note that there isn't one ideal home computer, because features vary from model to model. When it comes to making a final choice, you'll have to decide what's right for you.

Home computers come in desktop and handheld models, in many sizes and shapes—choose the one that's best for you.

Is the Computer Easy to Use? How much time and effort has the manufacturer spent in making the computer "user-friendly"? Does the keyboard have a standard typewriter-style keyboard, or are the keys arranged differently? If you're an experienced typist and will be using your machine for lots of writing, it's essential that the keys be placed in groupings you're familiar with.

If you're buying a console computer with a video display built in, make sure the screen is easy to read; a poorly designed video display can cause eyestrain after a few hours' use. Some home computers without full-color capabilities come with a green-tinted screen that's much easier on the eyes.

If the computer model you're interested in hooks up to an ordinary television set, make sure you see what the picture looks like. For various technical reasons, characters on a television set's screen can't be as sharp as they would be on a video display or video monitor—and this means they can be hard to read. You may be better off buying a separate monitor for another reason, too—if there's only one television set in the family, remember that the computer may preempt somebody's favorite program.

How Much Memory Does It Have? For most home uses, you'll need at least 16K of RAM memory. The ROM capacity, since it doesn't affect the way you use the computer, is less important; but be sure the computer is programmed to understand BASIC. You may also want to add memory later, so check to see whether this is possible with the computer you're looking at. Make sure the computer will be as usable in the future as it is now.

Is a Wide Range of Peripherals Available? Can you upgrade the computer after you buy it? For example, you should be able to buy:

Look for a computer that has a wide range of peripherals available — even if you don't want them now, you may decide to add a disk drive, extra memory, a printer, and other accessories later.

- A cassette tape recorder.
- Floppy disk drives.
- A printer.
- Additional memory.
- A bigger or better video display.
- Other accessories (dust covers, stands and tables, tape and disk file cases, etc.).

Is Software Readily Available? How wide a range of software is available for the brand of home computer? Does this software meet your needs? If you're going to use your computer for a home business, for example, and what's available is mostly game software, you're in for some problems.

What's the Documentation Like? Because a home computer is a rather complicated appliance, we haven't yet reached the point where anyone can just sit down at a computer and start using it. You have to follow the instructions — and this means that the documentation, the instruction manuals that come with the computer, are extremely important. Look at the documentation before you buy. Is the manual easy to follow? Is it written in plain English, or is it written with lots of technical jargon that assumes you're a computer expert? No matter how good a computer is otherwise, it's useless if you can't figure out how to use it.

Does It Have a Good Warranty? Although all computers have warranties because they are required by law, the length of the warranty may differ. Most computer warranties are 90 days, but some companies warranty their products for up to two years. Computers are complicated electronic gadgets, and things *will* go wrong. If you're going to be using your computer extensively, it's nice to know that the company will back it up.

Is the Manufacturer's Reputation Good? Just as some warranties are better than others, some manufacturers are better than others on helping you out with any problems you may have after you buy your machine. The best way to find out about the manufacturer's reputation is to talk with people who own home computers; word of mouth is still the most reliable indication of how good—or bad—a product is. Any reputable computer dealer should be happy to supply you with the names of owners of various brands. If the dealer won't give you references, watch out—it could mean the brand you're considering doesn't have a good reputation. A good source of advice on manufacturer reputation is a local computer club.

COMPARING DESKTOP COMPUTERS

Well over a million home computers are in use today. In the next few pages we'll look at a few popular examples of desktop home computers, made by several major manufacturers. Some of these companies make computers for both home and small business use, and some computers are suitable for both applications. Because new computers are being introduced all the time, the prices and specifications described here may change quickly. Remember, too, that list prices are often discounted. Use the information that follows as an introduction to the kinds of features and the capabilities now available.

Timex/Sinclair

Sinclair Research Limited, a British company, has made a name for itself in breaking new ground in consumer electronics. Clive Sinclair, the power behind Sinclair Research, introduced the first low-cost pocket calculators back in the early 1970s. Perhaps his most important breakthrough came several years ago when the company developed and sold portable television sets about the size of a paperback book.

Thanks to the phenomenal sales of Sinclair's ZX-81, a true low-cost computer, the company now claims to be "the world's largest manufacturer of personal computers." It may be true—there are about half a million ZX-81s in use.

The Timex/Sinclair 1000. The Sinclair ZX-81 computer has always been manufactured by Timex, a company best known for its watches; and Timex has recently taken over the distribution of the ZX-81 in the United States. This computer is now called the Timex/Sinclair 1000. The price has been reduced from about $150 to about $100, and the computer is

The Timex/Sinclair 1000 is a true low-cost computer. It's also powerful, and it has moving graphics, single-key entry, mathematical functions, and error detection. It hooks up to a home television set.

scheduled to be available at thousands of retail outlets, ranging from grocery stores to discount department stores.

When it comes to home computers, you usually get what you pay for, and not much else. The Timex/Sinclair 1000 is a refreshing exception. Despite its low price tag, the 1000 is a powerful computer—not just a glorified calculator. Its 40-key *membrane keyboard*—a flat piece of plastic with imprinted key tops and labels — lacks the professional touch of nearly all the other computers we talk about here, but the computer has powerful capabilities, including moving graphics, single-key entry of many BASIC commands, mathematical functions often not found on much more expensive computers, and error detection every time you type in a line of BASIC. It weighs only 12 ounces.

The Timex/Sinclair 1000 can't produce color images, but it hooks up to a home television set—either black-and-white or color. The computer displays 24 lines of up to 32 characters — uppercase only — on the screen, and a cable is included so you can save programs on any cassette tape recorder.

Software for the 1000 is sold by Timex, Sinclair, and a variety of independent companies. Because most of it comes on cassette tape, it's relatively inexpensive — usually $10 to $20. Although the basic computer unit comes with only 2K of RAM, it can be expanded to 18K with a $100 plug-in memory expansion module. The company is also planning to offer a $100 dot-matrix printer.

The Timex/Sinclair 1000 certainly qualifies as the best bargain around in personal computers. Because it has limitations, it's far from being a professional machine, but it's an ideal computer if you're interested in getting started in computing.

Other Timex/Sinclair Computers. Besides the 1000, Timex/Sinclair also hopes to market a $250 computer called the Spectrum soon. This model has all the features of the 1000, plus more RAM memory, full-color graphics, a keyboard with push-buttons, and miniature floppy disk drives.

Commodore

Commodore was one of the first companies to get involved in personal computers. In 1976, it introduced the PET, the first low-cost desktop computer. The firm now makes a complete line of personal computers, ranging from the low-priced VIC-20 to more expensive business-oriented systems.

The VIC-20. At about $300, the VIC-20 is one of the

most inexpensive full-feature home computers available. It has a 60-key typewriter-style keyboard and is designed to be connected to any television set. The basic model has only 5K of RAM, but it can be expanded to 32K.

Pictures and characters can be displayed on the VIC-20 in up to 16 colors, and simple BASIC commands let you establish up to 255 combinations of screen and border colors. The VIC-20 is also a music machine: it has four built-in tone generators that cover five octaves, and a white-noise generator for creating music and sound effects.

Besides all the fancy sound and graphics, the VIC-20 displays both uppercase and lowercase letters, so you can use it for word processing. Unfortunately, it can display only 23 lines that are 22 characters wide — a far cry from the 32 to 80 characters per line that most other home computers can handle. But special editing keys allow you to insert and delete characters and words, and to move the cursor — the blinking square that shows where you are on the screen — around the screen. The VIC-20 also has four special-function keys that you can program to perform up to eight program steps, just by hitting a single key.

There's a wide range of software available for the VIC-20 — on both floppy disks and cassette tapes. Subjects include games, family finance, education, business, and word processing. A full line of peripherals is also available. The VIC 1515 graphic printer costs about $400; there's also a floppy disk drive — the VIC 1540, priced at about $600 — which stores up to 170K of data on a 5¼-inch minifloppy disk. You can't use just any cassette tape recorder with the VIC-20; you have to buy Commodore's. The C2N Datassette recorder costs about $75.

The VIC-20 has a socket that allows you to plug in

accessories like a joystick or light pen. The company also offers a variety of plug-in cartridges for expanding the VIC's standard 5K memory. Other cartridges let you connect accessories, including a modem — the VIC 1600 VICMODEM cartridge, priced at about $110—it's for hooking the computer up to a telephone line.

Other Commodore Computers. Recently, Commodore introduced its model 64 computer. At about $600, this model comes with 64K RAM. It can display 25 lines, 40 characters wide—both uppercase

The Commodore VIC-20, top, is one of the least expensive full-feature home computers on the market. The Model 64, bottom, comes with 64K of RAM.

and lowercase. This computer can use the VIC-20 peripherals.

At the other end of the spectrum is the Commodore CBM, a computer designed specifically for small business applications like word processing, accounting, and inventory control. Priced at around $1,500, the CBM includes 32K of RAM—which can be expanded to 96K—and a built-in video screen that displays a full 80-character line, the standard for business applications.

The Commodore CBM, designed for small business use, displays a full 80-character line on its screen.

Commodore's top-of-the-line computer is the SuperPET, a $2,000 machine with 96K of RAM. The SuperPET has many advanced features, including many computer languages such as COBOL, FORTRAN, and Pascal.

Texas Instruments

Texas Instruments, well known for its handheld calculators, is a major manufacturer of the chips other computer makers use in their computers — if you looked under the cover of just about any personal computer, there's a good chance you'd find at least some TI chips. The company also makes a line of high-priced computers and terminals for professional, business, and industrial use.

The TI 99/4A. Texas Instruments' home computer is called the 99/4A — an improved successor to the

Texas Instruments' home computer is the 99/4A, with 16K of RAM and a 16-bit microprocessor. The 99/4A is intended for first-time computerists, but it's powerful enough for the more experienced, too.

99/4, the company's first home computer. The 99/4A has 16K of RAM and the same advanced 16-bit microprocessor found in the company's larger business computers. The suggested retail price of the TI 99/4A is about $450, but this price is heavily discounted by some dealers. Texas Instruments says that the TI 99/4A is intended for first-time home computer users, but its advanced capabilities also make it a good choice for more experienced computerists. The 99/4A is primarily designed to be used with plug-in "Command Modules"—cartridges that plug into the front of the computer. A wide range of software is available on these cartridges, including tax and investment record-keeping, securities analysis, household budget management, nutrition, and personal record-keeping. Many games and educational

The TI 99/4A is primarily designed to be used with plug-in cartridges called "Command Modules."

modules are also available. Texas Instruments also offers a floppy disk drive, for which additional, more sophisticated, software is available. All this ability doesn't come cheap: the PHP 1850 disk drive costs about $500, and to use it, you also need the PHP 1800 controller, which costs about $300.

The 99/4A features color graphics, with up to 16 colors available. A built-in sound generator, for music and sound effects, covers up to five octaves. For the best picture, the company recommends a high-quality 10-inch video display, which sells for about $400. The 99/4A can also be connected to any TV set, with a $40 *video modulator*.

A full line of accessories is available for the 99/4A. The PHP 2500 impact printer costs about $750; the PHP 1600 modem costs about $225. One of the most interesting accessories is a speech synthesizer that lets the computer "speak" with a vocabulary of some 300 words — about $125. The computer's built-in RAM can be expanded from 16K to 48K for about $300.

Radio Shack

Radio Shack, your friendly neighborhood electronics store, is credited with getting the home computer revolution rolling. The TRS-80 Model I, introduced in 1977, was the first generally available low-cost home computer designed specifically for personal use. Radio Shack now makes a full line of personal computers, and supports them with a wide range of accessories and software. Radio Shack computers and software are available only in Radio Shack stores, but there are many of these retail outlets across the country.

The TRS-80 Color Computer. The TRS-80 Color Computer is a reasonably priced machine — under

$400—that's designed primarily for home use. It has 4K of RAM, but more powerful models with extended color graphics capabilities are also available. The Color Computer can display eight colors and 16 lines of up to 32 characters, but in uppercase only.

Although floppy disk drives and cassette tape recorders are available for the Color Computer, the machine can also use plug-in cartridges. A wide range of cartridges is available, including games, home finance, and word processing. The CTR-80A cassette recorder is available for about $60; a mini-disk drive costs about $600. The Model VII line

Radio Shack's TRS-80 Color Computer can display eight colors; a wide range of software is available.

printer sells for about $400, and a direct-connect modem is available for about $150.

The TRS-80 Model III. This is the workhorse of the Radio Shack line of home computers. It's unique among the computers we describe here because it's an all-in-one package—it has an attached keyboard and a built-in 12-inch black-and-white video display. Up to two floppy disk drives, which are optional, can be installed in slots next to the video display. The Disk Drive Kit 1 sells for about $850.

In appearance, the Model III resembles an office desktop computer more than a typical home computer. The $1,000 price of the basic Model III, with 16K of RAM that can be expanded to 48K, makes it a very good buy. The 65-key typewriter-style keyboard gives you a full uppercase and lowercase character set, and the video screen displays 16 lines of 32

The TRS-80 Model III from Radio Shack is an all-in-one package, with 16K of RAM and a huge variety of software.

characters, including special graphics symbols and special alphabets, in black and white.

Radio Shack and a number of independent companies supply a huge variety of software for the Model III; it's one of the most widely supported computers around. Accessories available for the Model III include several models of modems, an appliance-control system, cassette tape recorders, floppy disk drives, and one of the widest ranges of printers available from a personal computer company.

Other Radio Shack Computers. The Radio Shack computer line also includes two powerful personal computers designed for serious business use. The TRS-80 Model II sells for about $3,500, and has a wide range of professional software. The Model 16 is one of the first small business computers to use a 16-bit microprocessor—that's where the "Model 16" comes from. Such power doesn't come cheap, though—the Model 16 is priced at about $5,000.

Atari

Just about everybody knows the Atari name; the company is famous for its arcade and home video games. Atari is one of the world's largest manufacturers of microprocessor-based home entertainment products. The company has sold millions of its home video game systems, which are essentially sophisticated home computers without a keyboard.

The Atari 800. This computer, which sells for about $900, is Atari's entry into the home computer market. It can be connected to any home TV.

As you might expect from Atari's sophisticated games, the video graphics and sound effects of games for the Atari 800 are phenomenal—far and away the best of any of the personal computers. The

The Atari 800, from the maker of the famous video games, has exceptionally good color graphics and sound effects. It also has 16K of RAM, which can be expanded to 64K, and a full range of peripherals.

800 produces 16 colors, each with 16 intensities, and displays 24 lines of 40 characters — both uppercase and lowercase. The 800 has a 57-key typewriter-like keyboard.

The 800 is more than just a game computer. It has 16K of RAM, which can be expanded to 48K with plug-in modules. Atari also makes a full line of peripherals and accessories for the 800. There's the 810 floppy disk drive at about $600, the 825 printer for $800, the 830 acoustic modem at about $200, and both paddle-type and joystick controllers at about $20 to $25 a pair. A special cassette tape recorder is required for use with cassette tapes; the Atari 410 recorder costs about $100.

There's less software available for the 800 than for some other popular home computers, but Atari sells a wide range of software in cassette tape, floppy disk, and plug-in cartridge form. Programs include music composition, word processing, stock analysis, personal financial management, investment analysis, conversational French and Spanish, touch-typing, and—as you'd expect—a wide variety of games.

The Atari 400. The Atari 400 is the 800's less expensive counterpart. At about $300, it's considerably cheaper than the 800. Like the Timex/Sinclair 1000

The Atari 400 has 16K of RAM, and can handle the full range of Atari software on cassettes and cartridges.

home computer, it has a flat plastic membrane keyboard that lacks raised keys. The 16K 400, which can't be expanded as far as its RAM memory is concerned, doesn't take most of the 800's accessories; but it can handle all the sophisticated Atari software on tape cassettes and plug-in cartridges. Like the 800, the Atari 400 requires a special cassette tape recorder; the Atari 410 recorder costs about $100.

IBM

Everybody knows the IBM name — it's usually the first one that comes to mind when the word "computer" is mentioned. For years, IBM was known for the highest-quality and most innovative business computer products. But the company held off on introducing a personal computer until it was sure there was actually a market for them. Today, you can use an IBM at home as well as at the office.

The IBM Personal Computer. The IBM Personal Computer was finally introduced in mid-1981. It immediately caused a stir as one of the most professionally designed personal computers ever.

The separate typewriter-style 83-key keyboard of the IBM Personal Computer is easily one of the best available — what more would you expect from a company famous for its typewriters? It includes 10 special-function keys that you can program to perform a number of steps, and a handy 10-key numeric keypad for entering lots of numbers, as on a calculator. All keys are repetitive — when you hold them down, they'll repeat the character.

The computer carries its microprocessor, memory, and optional floppy disk drives in a *system unit*—a separate box to which you attach the keyboard and video display with cables. This lets you set up the system so it's most comfortable for you. Both black-

IBM's Personal Computer, with 16K of RAM that can be expanded to 256K, is expected to become the standard for the industry; its capabilities are exceptional. A full range of software and accessories is available.

and-white and color video displays are available, displaying 25 lines of 80 characters—uppercase and lowercase—in type styles that are very easy on the eyes. You can also mix text and graphics on the screen, and can display 16 colors.

At first glance, the IBM Personal Computer, with 16K of RAM, looks low-priced—but there's a catch. The $1,265 price for the basic unit includes only the keyboard and the basic microprocessor; IBM stuck with its "big system" roots by pricing everything separately, and a full system costs between $3,000 and $5,000, depending on what you get. This computer's RAM memory can be expanded to 256K!

All sorts of accessories and software are available for the IBM Personal Computer, both from the company and from independent suppliers. A dot-matrix printer costs about $550; a 160K disk drive costs about $450. More and more software will be available in the years to come. This computer is expected to become the standard by which other personal computers are measured.

Apple

The personal computer field was pioneered by a number of companies that sold kit computers to electronics hobbyists. Apple Computer was one of these firms.

From its start in a garage in the mid-1970s, Apple has grown to become one of the world's largest personal computer companies. And the Apple II is one of the world's largest-selling computers.

The Apple II. The Apple II, priced at about $1,350, looks like a long, narrow typewriter, and is designed to be connected to a television set. It's supplied with 16K of RAM, which can be expanded to 48K, and has a built-in connection for a cassette tape recorder.

More accessories and more software are available for the Apple II than for any other personal computer. A whole cottage industry has grown up around it; literally thousands of programs and hundreds of plug-in add-ons can be purchased.

Despite its phenomenal popularity, the Apple II has a few peculiarities. The strangest is the 52-key keyboard, which, although it resembles a standard typewriter, has many keys placed in strange locations. The Apple also displays uppercase characters only—so if you want to use it for word processing, you'll need to buy accessory circuit boards to give it this capability. The Apple II displays 24 lines of 40 characters; accessories are available that can extend this to 80 characters. The computer also has high-quality color graphics capabilities — it can display up to 15 colors—and a built-in tone generator.

A unique feature of the Apple II is that its circuitry

The Apple II, one of the most popular home computers, has an outstanding range of software and accessories.

is very easy to get to—not a consideration for everyday use, but a definite advantage when it comes to adding memory. Most other computer companies build their products so you won't be tempted to peek inside, but the Apple II's lid pops off to reveal eight slots for accessory circuit boards and other plug-in extras.

The Apple III is the most powerful Apple computer, designed for business uses like word processing.

Apple and other companies sell a variety of special plug-in accessories for the Apple II, including additional RAM memory, 80-character and lowercase text adapters, voice synthesizers, digital clocks, modems, joysticks, and a host of others. In fact, electronics hobbyists are fond of building their own Apple circuit boards. The Apple Disk II Drive with interface modem costs about $650; the Silentype Printer, a dot-matrix model, costs about $400.

The Apple III. The Apple III is the firm's most powerful computer. This model, whose price starts at about $3,500, is aimed primarily at serious business and professional users. It has more built-in capabilities than the Apple II, and it has all the ease of use and ease of expansion that have made the Apple II one of the best-selling personal computers.

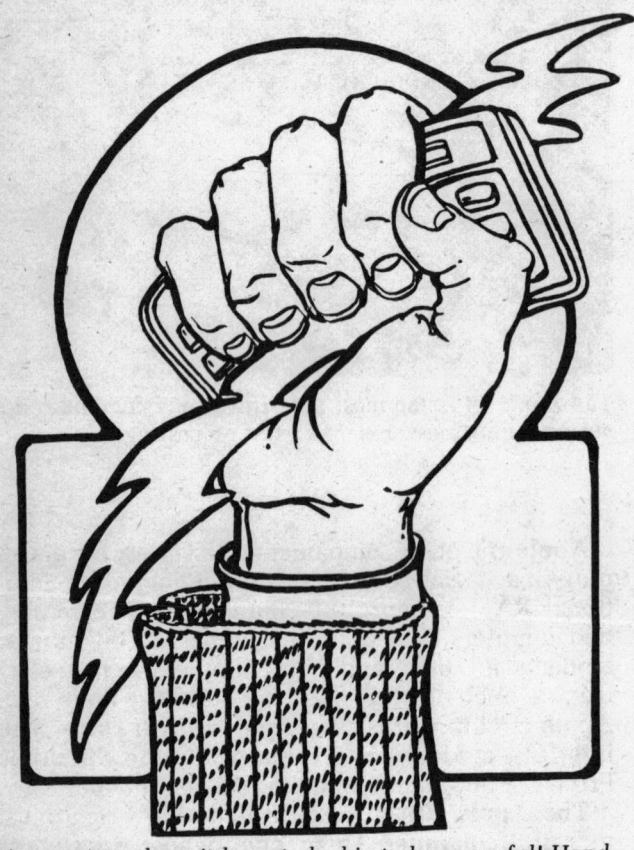

A computer doesn't have to be big to be powerful! Handheld computers give you true computer capability, in a package small enough to hold in your hand. More handheld computers are sure to come in the future.

COMPARING HANDHELD COMPUTERS

A computer you can hold in your hand or slip into a pocket is a lot more personal than its desktop counterparts. Several different handheld computers are now available, and their number will grow in the coming years. Here are a couple of representative examples.

Sharp PC-1500/Radio Shack TRS-80 PC-2

The Sharp PC-1500 is far from being just a glorified calculator; it's a true computer, with lots of power in a package that slips easily into a coat pocket. It's $7^{11}/_{16}$ by 1 by $3^3/_8$ inches in size, and weighs only 13

Radio Shack's TRS-80 PC-2 can use cassettes and plug-in memory cartridges; a wide range of software is available.

ounces. A nearly identical computer is also available from Radio Shack, where it's known as the TRS-80 PC-2. This version has a slightly different keyboard.

The basic PC-1550/PC-2 pocket computer model sells for about $300, and includes 2.64K of RAM that can be expanded to 11.5K by plugging a RAM cartridge into the bottom of the machine. Information typed into the computer's miniature 65-key typewriter-style keyboard is shown one line at a time on a 26-character dot-matrix liquid crystal display— a larger version of the displays used on digital watches. A unique feature of the display is that the 1,092 dots on it can be individually controlled to provide custom-designed characters and graphics. Both uppercase and lowercase letters are also displayed.

The PC-1500/PC-2 also has a built-in clock/calendar that can be programmed as an alarm clock, with a built-in beeper. You can also program primitive music by specifying the length and frequency of the beeps.

The PC-1500/PC-2 can be used with any cassette tape recorder, but a special Sharp recorder, the CE-152, is also available; it sells for about $100. The Radio Shack Minisette-9 tape recorder sells for about $80. One exciting accessory from Sharp—also available for the Radio Shack computer — is the CE-150 printer and cassette interface. This remarkable peripheral, a $250 option, is essentially a tray into which you slide the pocket computer, that allows you to load and save programs on cassette tape. The printer is unique. About the size of a bar of soap, it has four miniature ballpoint pens — black, blue, green, and red — installed in a revolving cylinder that slides back and forth across the paper. You can instruct it to print characters in any of the four colors, and in nine different sizes. You can also draw

The Sharp PC-1500, with the same capabilities as the TRS-80 PC-2, is far from being a glorified calculator. One exciting accessory is a printer, which produces printed characters, graphs, and even drawings.

lines, and with a little patience, you can create your own computerized drawings. You can even do simple word processing tasks like making address labels and name tags.

A wide range of software is available for both the Sharp PC-1500 and the Radio Shack PC-2, including programs on tape cassettes and plug-in cartridges. This little powerhouse gives you just a hint of the advanced capabilities tomorrow's portable computers will have.

Quasar/Panasonic HHC

The HHC (Hand Held Computer) from Quasar/Panasonic is a sophisticated portable computer with programming features more sophisticated than some full-size home computers offer. Manufactured in Japan by one of the world's largest electronics companies, the HHC measures 8$^{5}/_{16}$ by 1$^{3}/_{16}$ by 3$^{3}/_{4}$ inches; it weighs 21 ounces. It comes with either 4K or 8K or RAM, which can be expanded to 16K. In addition, up to three ROM capsules with applications software can be installed in special sockets inside the computer. The basic unit—without extra memory—sells for about $525.

Unlike other handheld computers, the HHC has a miniature 65-key typewriter-style keyboard. It has a

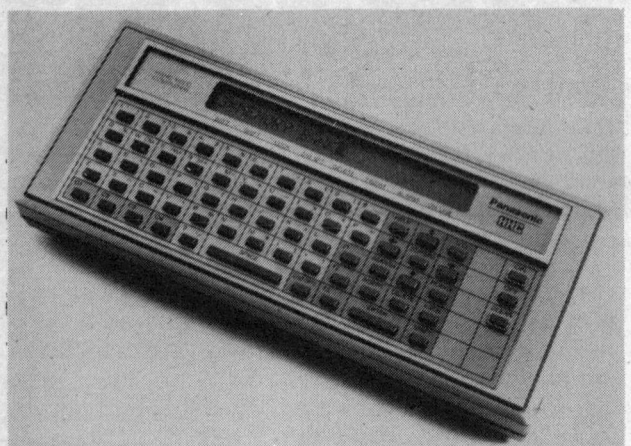

Quasar/Panasonic's HHC is a sophisticated handheld with more advanced features than some full-size computers. It comes with 4K or 8K of RAM, which can be expanded to 16K; applications software can also be installed.

26-character dot-matrix liquid crystal display with both uppercase and lowercase characters. Built into the HHC are five main functions that appear on a menu—just pick one and press the appropriate button. Besides having built-in BASIC and a file system for storing information, the HHC also uses SNAP, another high-level language. The HHC can also be used as an advanced calculator and, with appliance interfaces, as a clock/controller to turn appliances on and off.

Quasar/Panasonic makes a line of miniature peripherals specifically for the HHC. These include the RLP 1003 thermal printer, which sells for about $225, and the RL-P2001 television interface, which sells for about $350. When used with a color TV, the HHC displays up to eight colors. A programmable

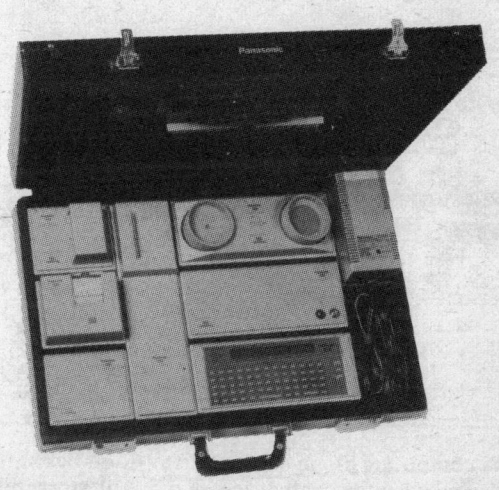

A full line of miniature peripherals is available for Quasar/Panasonic's HHC handheld computer.

acoustic modem, the RL-P4001, is also available; it sells for under $300. And Quasar/Panasonic makes an AC adapter/recharger, the RD-9498, for about $60.

WHERE TO BUY YOUR COMPUTER

Although deciding which home computer to buy is one of the most difficult choices you'll have to make, *where* to buy can also be a challenge. Just as with the computer systems themselves, you have many choices, and your decision can affect both the price you pay and the service you receive.

Home computers are now sold in thousands of stores across the country, ranging from discount department stores to full-line computer centers. Many computers are also available by mail order, and there's a thriving market for bargain-priced used computers. Each of these options has its advantages

Home computers are available in stores all over the country, from discount centers to department stores, by mail order and in full-line computer stores. Check out all your options before you buy.

and disadvantages, and it pays to look at all the possibilities before you buy.

Retail Department Stores

It wasn't very long ago that if you told a department store clerk you wanted to see a computer, he'd give you a very strange look. But over the past couple of years, home computers have become a true consumer electronics item—they've taken their place on department store shelves, next to the pocket calculators, digital watches, and personal portable cassette tape recorders. The major mass merchandisers like Sears Roebuck; J.C. Penney; and Montgomery Ward have already started selling home computers, and with the introduction of the Timex/Sinclair 1000, you'll see home computers almost everywhere.

Because they can buy in volume, retail department stores and retailers often sell computers for well below their list price. But there are a couple of disadvantages to buying a home computer from them. One problem is lack of knowledge on the salesperson's part. Computers are complicated machines, and it requires both knowledge and skill to sell them. Early experiments with selling home computers in department stores failed because the stores often just displayed the computers next to the calculators and told the salespeople to "sell them." Happily, the problem of inadequate sales knowledge is rapidly being solved; as home computers become more and more popular, many stores are starting their own computer departments and staffing them with specially trained salespeople.

Another possible disadvantage is limited choice. Most retail stores can't carry as wide a variety of computers and accessories as a store that sells nothing else. This too will change as home computers become more and more popular. But for the time being, if you want to buy your home computer from a department store, you'll probably have to visit several stores to see a wide variety.

Service can be a problem, too. Although most computer stores have their own service departments, retail department stores usually send a computer back to the manufacturer if there are any problems. This cuts both ways—factory service is the best service, but it can take time. If you're depending on your computer for critical business applications, you may not be able to wait the weeks that factory service requires, and even if you aren't depending on your machine, it's inconvenient to be without it.

Despite the disadvantages, buying your home computer from a department store can give you both a low price and a dependable product. If you want to buy locally and you have a good idea of what you want, a department store could be the place to go.

Mail Order

Like everything else these days, computers are available by mail-order. You can buy an entire computer system by mail or even by telephone, and have it delivered to your door. If you're sure about what home computer you want to buy, mail order can be an excellent way to buy your system. Not only is the choice of products wide, but the prices are usually the lowest. There are, however, some hazards to watch out for.

First, make sure you buy from an established, reputable firm. Some mail-order companies announce a "spectacular" new product months before it's ready to be shipped. Hundreds of people send in thousands of dollars and then wait—sometimes for a long time. Before you order anything by mail, find out about the reputation of the company involved. Read computer magazines, ask at computer clubs, and try to find someone who's actually purchased something from the company. Most mail-order houses should also be happy to supply you with the names of some of their customers. If they won't, be cautious.

Second, make sure you know exactly what you want when you place your order. If you get the product number wrong or write the description inaccurately, you may receive the wrong item. Follow all the ordering and shipping instructions exactly to be sure your order is processed correctly.

Finally, it's important to note that you are responsible for checking out the computer system when it arrives. Most mail-order houses send out unopened boxes, straight from the manufacturer. Most of the time, the computer will work properly — the computer industry has a well-deserved reputation for strict quality control. But what happens if the machine is broken or doesn't work? Make sure you find out the mail-order company's policy on replacing defective equipment. Some companies will replace the equipment, but some may require you to send it back to the factory for warranty service — often a time-consuming process.

Computer Stores

Although department stores and mail-order companies are excellent sources of home computer equipment, most people still buy their systems at one of the more than 2,000 computer stores located throughout the United States. The world's first personal computer store opened in 1975 in Santa Monica, California. It was scoffed at by the "experts," but the concept of computer stores exploded as personal computers became more and more popular. Today, you're sure to find a computer store in every major metropolitan area.

Whether you're buying or just looking, a computer store gives you several benefits. Because they sell only computers, these stores usually have on display a full selection of computers, accessories, and software. You can compare the features and advantages of the different computers you're interested in, and you can actually try out the machines—the best way to shop for a home computer.

You'll also usually find the most knowledgeable salespeople in computer stores. They can give you solid advice on what you need, and can help you solve your special problems. Watch out, though, for stores where the salespeople are so knowledgeable that they talk in computer jargon instead of in plain English. The first computer stores catered to computer hobbyists — people who build their own equipment and write long programs in assembly language, for fun. There are still some of those stores out there, but they're rapidly disappearing as computers become true products for average consumers.

Most computer stores carry a full line of peripherals and extras like printers, floppy disk drives, modems, and so on. And they'll usually let you try before you buy. These stores also usually offer special services, like making up special cable connections and helping to get a nonstandard accessory working with a customer's computer.

Computer stores win hands-down when it comes to servicing and supporting the machines they sell. Many stores have their own service departments. If you depend on your computer for a business or professional application, quick turnaround on service can be a life-saver. And many computer stores will offer you equipment to use while they service yours.

What about disadvantages? The main one is price. You might be able to negotiate a 5 to 10 percent discount for the purchase of a complete system, but in most cases, you'll pay the full retail price for equipment bought at a computer store. This is because computer stores give you attentive after-the-sale extras such as as service, and because they can't buy computers in thousands of units the way big retail chains can.

Just as with any retail business, there are a few unscrupulous operators. Before you do business with a computer store, check its reputation by asking for the names of customers and by checking with the Better Business Bureau. The members of a local computer club or users' group, again, are probably your best source for sound advice.

Despite their higher prices, you should definitely consider buying your system from a local computer store, especially if you'll be using it for business applications. It's nice to know there's someone you can call any time a problem or question crops up.

USED COMPUTERS

If your budget is tight, and you want or need a better computer system than a low-priced "entry-level" machine, you might consider buying a used computer. Because new models are appearing all the time, older computer models are being traded in or sold as their owners move up to new machines.

Computer stores often sell used computers — machines traded in by their customers for newer units. You can also find classified listings of used computers in computer magazines, in computer club and users' group newsletters, and even in the local newspaper. The problem, of course, is the same as with used cars — you never really know what you're

The computer market is changing fast, and used computers are often traded in for new models and resold. Buying a used computer is risky — there's no warranty. The rule is simple: stay with well-known brands.

getting. A used computer may be a perfectly good machine; on the other hand, it may have serious problems. You just don't know, until it's too late.

If you do decide that a used computer is for you, be careful. Warranty protection is virtually nonexistent on used computers—and computers can be very expensive to repair. Make sure any used computer is one of the well-known and reputable brands, like the ones mentioned earlier in this chapter. A couple of years ago, there were a number of computer lines that made their brief appearance in the marketplace and then disappeared for good. Because their manufacturers are out of business, service is now almost impossible to get. The rule for buying a used machine is simple: if you've never heard of the manufacturer, stay away.

Before buying a used computer, it's essential that you check it out thoroughly. The best way to do this is to take along a knowledgeable friend — maybe a fellow member of your local computer club — to give the machine some testing. Make sure it's working perfectly before you buy it. Computer stores are required by consumer protection laws to refund your money within a certain period of time if a used com-

Before you buy a used computer, look it over carefully — have a knowledgeable computerist give it some testing. Make sure the computer is working perfectly before you close the deal.

puter doesn't work, but this is not the case with private sales—once you buy a lemon, you're stuck with it. Thorough testing is essential to eliminate this possibility.

BUILDING A COMPUTER

The personal computer started out as a toy for dedicated electronics hobbyists — people who like to build their own equipment. You sent in your check to one of several computer companies and got back a kit—a box full of parts and a few pages of instructions. The rest was up to you and your soldering iron.

Today, the vast majority of computers are factory-assembled and tested. But just as some people like to build radios, televisions, and other electronic products from kits, you may also like the idea of building your own computer. It isn't foolproof—but it can be done.

Building a computer kit and having your machine work fine the first time you plug it in is a rewarding experience; the feeling of accomplishment is unsurpassed. But that's not always the way it is. You should never try to build a computer from a kit unless you've had previous kit-building experience. If you're interested, start with a couple of low-priced electronics kits — like a digital alarm clock, for instance—to get a feel for whether you'd like to tackle the chore of building a kit computer. You'll have to know how to solder delicate components correctly, and you'll have to have patience.

The world's largest manufacturer of electronic kits is the Heath Company. Heath makes several computer kits that can save you 25 to 30 percent of the cost of buying a fully assembled and tested unit. Heath's instructions and packaging have a reputation as being the best in the industry, and the company will give assistance to anyone who has problems building one of its kits. Be warned, though; building some computers is a time-consuming and often boring undertaking that could tie up your evenings for a couple of months. Even the best kit-builders occasionally make mistakes, and tracking down the problems can be difficult. Mistakes are especially likely if you're an inexperienced kit-builder, or if you try to hurry things along because you're anxious to use the computer.

BUYING RIGHT: HOW TO MAKE YOUR CHOICE

Once you've definitely decided to buy your own home computer, it's wise to pause and rethink your choices. There's hardware and software in plenty out there, but somewhere is the one computer that's right for you. Take your time. A computer is an investment—of time, of money, of interest. Make sure you get the best investment possible—your trouble will pay off when you use your new computer. We've covered a lot of ground in this chapter, but the right way to buy can be summarized in a few simple steps:
1. Decide what you want to do with your computer.
2. Find the models that will fit your needs.
3. Compare them by getting hands-on demonstrations.
4. Find out about service after the sale.
5. Then make your choice—and enjoy!

Chapter 6

You don't have to be a superbrain to program a computer! Programming isn't essential, but it can be fun — follow these simple steps into the world of BASIC, and you'll be writing your own programs in no time.

The ABCs of Programming

IF YOU'RE like most people who haven't had any experience with computers, you're probably worried about learning to program a home computer. Let us put your mind to rest—you don't have to know how to program to use a home computer; you can buy an almost unlimited supply of ready-to-run software developed by expert programmers, or use ready-written programs published in books and magazines. And commercial programs really lead you by the hand—when you run a packaged program, the computer will display instructions and ask you questions. All you have to do is type your answers or choices into the keyboard.

If you're not interested in learning how computers are programmed, you could skip this chapter. But

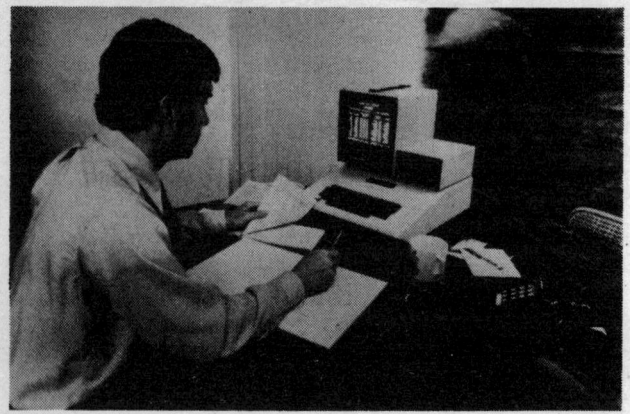
It looks hard, but programming a computer is just giving it a list of simple, step-by-step instructions.

before you do, think about this: you already have some programming experience!

Consider the pay telephone. Before you can talk with the person you want to call, you have to follow a simple list of instructions:

1. Look up the number of the person you want to call in a telephone directory.
2. Remove the telephone's handset from its cradle.
3. Insert the proper amount of money in coins.
4. Wait for a dial tone.
5. Dial the number you want, or push the proper buttons.

This list of instructions seems so simple that you're probably wondering why we've included it. The reason, of course, is that the instructions are a simple program. Though it's designed for use by a person, it's just as much a program as the ones designed for use by computers. And telephone programs are not the only ones you use — you also use programs to operate many other kinds of devices and machines, ranging from washing machines and ovens—the microwave oven is the best example—to thermostats and jukeboxes. And you use mental programs to perform everyday tasks such as cooking, writing a letter, playing a game, and planning a vacation.

When it comes right down to it, programming is

Programming a computer is like making a telephone call; just follow a simple list of instructions.

really just logical thinking. It's an indispensable part of most of our daily lives. So why are so many people intimidated by computer programming? Maybe the science-fiction image of the computer as a super-intelligent electronic brain is partially responsible for this feeling, but whatever its cause, the fear is ill-founded. Programming can be downright easy — and it can also be a lot of fun. By the time you finish reading this chapter, you'll be well acquainted with the fundamentals of BASIC, the most common programming language — and the easiest — used by home computers. As you'll soon see, BASIC is so simple that a beginner can start to write programs within a few hours — with or without a computer!

GETTING DOWN TO *BASIC*

As we've pointed out in earlier chapters, BASIC — Beginner's All-purpose Symbolic Instruction Code — is a high-level computer language that lets you use ordinary words, phrases, symbols, and numbers to give orders to a computer. Like any other language, BASIC has a vocabulary of words, and these words have very precise meanings. Because it's a two-way language, BASIC can be used to simulate conversations between you and your computer. And it produces various messages that tell you when your computer is ready for new instructions and when you've given it incorrect instructions.

The best way to learn BASIC is to try some actual computer programs written in this easy language. Although having a home computer in front of you would be helpful, you really don't need one to learn. This chapter will teach you some of the basics of BASIC, with the help of an imaginary home computer. There are slight differences in the various versions or dialects of BASIC used by various brands of

Even without a computer in front of you, you can learn to "talk" BASIC—the high-level computer language that lets you use ordinary words, symbols, and numbers to tell your computer what to do.

computers, but the one we'll use is representative of them all.

A SIMPLE *BASIC* PROGRAM

Complicated equations and long strings of numbers flash through the minds of most people when the word "computer" is mentioned. Because much of the information in this book is based on the fact that the operation of computers is based on binary numbers, let's work with a simple BASIC program to change the "number-crunching" image computers have.

When you first switch your imaginary home computer on, the video display screen will say:

READY
≻

Real computers usually display this brief message or a similar one.

READY is called a *prompt*. It tells you that your computer is ready for instructions, beginning at the screen's location indicated by ≻. The dash is called a *cursor*. It allows you to quickly locate where a character or symbol will appear on the screen after it has been entered from the keyboard.

Now you're ready to type the following information into the keyboard of your imaginary computer. Be sure to press the ENTER key after typing each line of the program—if you don't, the computer will keep waiting for more instructions. ENTER tells the computer, "That's it for this line; now be ready for the next one."

Your next commands are:

10 PRINT "WELCOME TO THE WORLD OF HOME COMPUTING!"
20 END

Did you make a mistake? No problem; just backspace to the error by pressing the key labeled with an arrow pointing to the left. Every time you press this key, the cursor will move one space to the left. When you reach the error, type in the correct letter or number. Want to retype a complete line? Just ignore the original line and begin a new line with the same number as the one you want to replace; the computer will automatically erase the original line for you.

Finished? Believe it or not, you've just typed a

genuine program into the computer. All you have to do to execute or run your program is to type:

RUN

Now hit the ENTER key. The computer will carry out the instruction in your program by showing on its screen:

WELCOME TO THE WORLD OF HOME COMPUTING!

This, of course, is a very simple program, but it does demonstrate several important rules about BASIC.

The first is that PRINT is a BASIC language term or statement that orders the computer to display everything — even spaces — enclosed by quotation marks following and on the same line as PRINT. You'll find PRINT statements to be among the most common of all BASIC operations.

The second rule is that a program should usually be concluded with an END statement. This prevents the computer from wandering down into the remnants of some other program that you may have previously entered into the computer.

The third rule is that the ENTER key must be pressed to load each line of a program into the computer's memory. This is very important. You can make it easy to remember by thinking of the ENTER key as the carriage-return key on a typewriter. In fact, some computer manufacturers label this key as RETURN or CR (Carriage Return).

Did you notice that the program consists of two lines of text and that each line is preceded by a number? Without the line numbers, the computer will not consider the information as part of a program.

Why are the lines numbered 10 through 20 instead

of 1 and 2? They can, in fact, be numbered 1 and 2. It's customary, however, to number the lines in a BASIC program 10, 20, 30, and so on, because this gives you plenty of room to insert extra numbers or steps into the program if you have to later on. For example, you might want to add steps 11, 12, and 13, or steps 21, 22, and 23.

Let's try it. Type the following line into your imaginary keyboard:

15 PRINT "COMPUTERS ARE DUMBER THAN YOU THINK."

Now type RUN and press ENTER. The screen will display:

WELCOME TO THE WORLD OR HOME COMPUTING!
COMPUTERS ARE DUMBER THAN YOU THINK.
READY
>-

Notice how the computer automatically inserted the new line into the correct place in your program? We know it did because the monitor's screen flashed the new line of type before displaying the READY prompt, indicating that it had reached the END statement. But we can prove it by using a BASIC command designated LIST. Type:

LIST

Now press ENTER, and the screen will display the complete program in numerical order:

>- **LIST**
10 PRINT "WELCOME TO THE WORLD OF HOME COMPUTING!"
15 PRINT "COMPUTERS ARE DUMBER THAN YOU THINK."
20 END
>-

As you can see, using the statement LIST tells the computer to display everything put into its memory. Moreover, the computer automatically processes the instructions in a program in numerical order—not in the order typed into the keyboard. As you'll see, this feature can save you lots of time.

So far, we've learned something about the following BASIC statements, prompts, and concepts: line numbers; ENTER; PRINT; quotation marks; END; RUN; and LIST.

Now let's liven up the program and learn about several important new features of BASIC by inserting a new line into our program. Type:

15 GOTO 10

Now press ENTER, type RUN, press ENTER again, and the entire screen will fill with lines that all read:

WELCOME TO THE WORLD OF HOME COMPUTING!

This new line has caused several major changes in our program. Let's cover each of them.

First, we've introduced GOTO, a new BASIC command. This statement on line 15 instructs the computer to immediately go to the designated line number, in this case 10, and do whatever is indicated. So GOTO sets up what's called a *loop*. The computer prints, "WELCOME TO THE WORLD OF HOME COMPUTING!" and then proceeds to the next instruction — which simply tells it to return to the first instruction. The result is an endless cycle as the computer continues to flash the specified sentence onto the screen.

The second thing we've done is to eliminate the

step we had earlier added to the program—15 PRINT "COMPUTERS ARE DUMBER THAN YOU THINK." We did this by simply using the original step's line number for the new step. This caused the computer to automatically erase the old step and remember the new one.

Still another thing we did is to make the END statement irrelevant because the computer never gets to it. But we'll leave it in because we're going to change the program again later.

Incidentally, computer programmers call GOTO an *unconditional transfer statement*. This definition is necessary to distinguish the GOTO statement from the so-called *conditional transfer statement*, designated IF...THEN.

Confused? Just remember that GOTO means the computer has no choice; it must go to the indicated line number. A computer programmer would say that GOTO transfers program control to the designated line. IF...THEN, as you've probably guessed, gives the computer an option. If a specified condition is met, then program control is transferred to a designated line number. Otherwise, the program continues its normal, step-by-step, line-by-line execution.

Using IF...THEN

IF...THEN doesn't make much sense without an explanation, so let's insert an IF...THEN statement in our simple demonstration program to see how it works. The screen of our imaginary computer is still displaying those rows of WELCOME TO THE WORLD OF HOME COMPUTING! so we'll have to press the BREAK key to stop the computer. Now let's type the following new steps into the keyboard, pressing ENTER after typing each line:

However smart your computer is, you're still the brains behind it. If...Then... is a conditional transfer statement — it gives the computer a choice. Your directions tell it which choice to make.

05 LET A = 0
12 LET A = 1 + X
13 IF A = 3 THEN 20

Now type RUN and press ENTER to start the program. The screen will display:

```
WELCOME TO THE WORLD OF HOME COMPUTING!
WELCOME TO THE WORLD OF HOME COMPUTING!
WELCOME TO THE WORLD OF HOME COMPUTING!
READY
>
```

As you can see, adding the three new lines ordered the computer to print the WELCOME message only three times before stopping. Can you figure out how the new program works?

Don't worry if you're in the dark. We've introduced a couple of new BASIC concepts, so let's explain them. First, type LIST and press ENTER to see the expanded program. The screen of the computer will display:

```
05 LET A = 0
10 PRINT "WELCOME TO THE WORLD OF HOME COMPUTING!"
12 LET A = 1 + A
13 IF A = 3 THEN 20
15 GOTO 10
20 END
```

Let's assume that we've typed RUN, and that we're following the program a step at a time as it's processed by the computer. Here's an explanation of what happens:

05 LET A = 0

This line introduces LET, another new member of BASIC's vocabulary. It simply establishes a memory location designated by any letter of the alphabet, and assigns the number on the right of the equal sign to this location. In this case, memory location A is assigned the value 0 (or cleared) in preparation for what takes place in line 12.

10 PRINT "WELCOME TO THE WORLD OF HOME COMPUTING!"

You already know what this line does.

12 LET A = 1 + A

This step seems to contradict itself. For example, if A = 5, then how can 5 = 1 + 5? Actually, this step isn't contradictory. Remember that LET assigns a number to a memory location, and in this case the location is designated A. Therefore, LET A = 1 + A just means that the number stored in A should be changed to the number now in A (which is 0) plus 1.

13 IF A = 3 THEN 20

Here's the IF...THEN statement that tells the computer how many times to run the program. Simply put, IF asks the question: "Is the number stored in memory location A a 3?" IF the answer is yes, THEN line 13 transfers program execution to line 20, which ends the program. Otherwise, the program continues to line 15, which it does because A only equals 1.

15 GOTO 10

This statement tells the program to return to line 10. The computer than flashes the message in line 10, advances to line 12, and adds another 1 to memory location A, which is now 0 + 1 + 1 or 2. It then continues to line 13, where it checks to see if the number in A is 3. It's not (A = 2), so the computer arrives at line 15, and the process continues. But the next time through the loop, the number in A reaches 3—every time the computer follows the loop, it adds another 1 to A. The third time through the loop, A will be 0 + 1 + 1 + 1, or 3. So, since A is now 3, the

IF of line 13 is fulfilled, and the THEN transfers program control to line 20.

20 END

The computer comes to a stop and flashes a READY after the three WELCOME messages.

Now do you understand how the expanded program works? If so, how would you order the computer to print ten WELCOME messages instead of three?

Well, if you changed line 13 to read IF A = 10 THEN 20, you're absolutely correct. And you're well on your way to understanding how the IF...THEN statement allows programs to establish various kinds of loops.

Incidentally, the number in A (IF A = ?) is called a variable by computer programmers. That's because it varies; it can be any number you select.

Loops can be very simple, like the one we've just studied. Or they can be more sophisticated, like this one. This loop orders the computer to display a screenful of random numbers:

```
05 CLS
06 LET Z = 0
10 PRINT RND (8); " ";
15 LET Z = Z + 1
16 IF Z = 240 THEN 30
20 GOTO 10
30 GOTO 30
```

When this program was run on a real computer, the following pattern of random numbers was flashed on the screen:

```
1431832788513188
6382863334766382
4521575441374338
4426147185442357
5528567818715563
3861771454585266
1563347635642512
8727432572711434
7431258631566658
3116444665842461
7278551462843336
3715857886361777
6664673841455136
6661523645651877
5155178445775372
>
```

This program introduces a couple of new BASIC terms, so let's see how it works.

05 CLS

This means "clear screen"—it removes everything already on the screen so that the full screen is available for your text. In this case, CLS isn't absolutely necessary because the extraneous material will be automatically removed from the screen as the lines of numbers are flashed on the screen. Its use here simply makes for a neater presentation of the random numbers.

06 LET Z = 0

This assigns a value of 0 to memory location Z.

10 PRINT RND (8) ; " " ;

RND is short for "random number." RND (8) converts the computer into an electronic "die" that automatically generates random numbers between 1 and 8, just as if a die were thrown on a table in a board game. Any number can be inserted inside the parentheses. For example, RND (100) would generate random numbers between 1 and 100.

PRINT tells the computer to flash the selected random number on the screen. The remainder of the line (; " " ;) tells the computer to "print" a single blank space after the selected random number; this separates the numbers.

The semicolons tell the computer to fill each line with random numbers and then proceed to the next line. Without ; " " ;, the screen would display a maximum of 16 random numbers in a single column along the left side of the screen.

```
15 Z = Z + 1
16 IF Z = 240 THEN 30
20 GOTO 10
```

These lines establish a loop that orders the computer to generate 240 random numbers. That's equivalent to 15 lines on the screen, containing 16 numbers each. When all 240 numbers are on the screen, the IF...THEN statement orders the program to move to line 30.

```
30 GOTO 30
```

This line is a "do-nothing" step. It tells the computer to establish a loop that seemingly does absolutely nothing! Actually, this step serves a useful purpose. If line 30 were an END statement, the screen would flash a READY prompt and erase two full lines of random numbers. GOTO 30 flashes only the cursor and erases none of the random numbers.

There's one catch about using a step like 30 GOTO 30. To enter new information, the computer's BREAK key must be pressed, because once the screen is full of random numbers the program will continue endlessly at line 30. BREAK is needed to tell it to stop.

Using FOR...NEXT To Establish Loops

How would you like to reduce the program that fills the computer screen with random numbers from seven to only five steps? A new BASIC expression called FOR...NEXT lets you do just that. Here's what the new version of the program looks like compared to the original one:

New Program (FOR...NEXT)
```
05 CLS
07 FOR Z = 1 TO 240
10 PRINT RND (8) ; " ";
15 NEXT Z
30 GOTO 30
```

Old Program (IF...THEN)
```
05 CLS
06 LET Z = 0
10 PRINT RND (8) ; " ";
15 LET Z = Z + 1
16 IF Z = 240 THEN 30
20 GOTO 10
30 GOTO 30
```

Both programs do exactly the same thing—fill the screen with 240 random numbers. Compare the two programs, however, and you'll see that the new program omits all four lines (lines 6, 15, 16, and 20) originally used to set up the loop that tells the computer to generate and print the random numbers.

The new program replaces the four lines associated with the IF...THEN expression of the original program with only two FOR...NEXT lines. Here's how the new program works:

```
05 CLS
07 FOR Z = 1 TO 240
```

Line 5 clears the screen, and line 7 stores a 1 in a memory location designated Z.

```
10 PRINT RND (8); " ";
15 NEXT Z
30 GOTO 30
```

Line 10 selects and prints a random number. Line 15 then orders a 1 to be added to the number in memory location Z. The cycle continues over and over again. After 240 random numbers have been displayed on the screen, line 15 is no longer valid, so the computer advances to the next line, which in this case is 30.

As you can see, FOR...NEXT can be much more efficient than IF...THEN. But IF...THEN is still very useful, particularly because the variable can be a number in any designated memory location; for example, IF A = B THEN 100. This can let you do some very clever programming tricks.

A very useful application for FOR...NEXT is as a so-called timer. The random-number programs we've been tinkering with are very fast. For example, the second one can fill the screen of a computer with 240 numbers in about six seconds! Suppose you want to slow down the computer a bit—in fact quite a bit, so that it flashes a new random number every

Programming is easy once you know the BASIC terms — just enter your commands and let the computer do the work.

second or so. The FOR...NEXT timer is the way to do this. Here's what the timer looks like:

12 FOR B = 1 TO 475
13 NEXT B

As you can see by the line numbers, the timer fits neatly between lines 10 and 15 of the short version of our random-number program. How does it work? Simple! When the computer reaches line 12, it places a 1 in a memory location called B. Line 13 then instructs the computer to return to line 12 and place a 2 in B. The process continues, all the while using up time, until the number in B is 475. The program then continues to the next random number selection. Result? The random numbers appear on the screen at about one-second intervals, thanks to the delay caused by the FOR...NEXT timer.

Another use for FOR...NEXT is in various kinds of programs involving arithmetic. We'll look at several of these applications later, but first, let's examine another very important role of the computer.

CONVERSATIONAL PROGRAMMING

Few features of computers are as impressive as their ability to carry on a "conversation." Naturally, the computer's side of the conversation has to be programmed. But the result can greatly simplify the use of a computer, because its screen can display instructions for you.

A key BASIC statement for conversational programs is INPUT. This statement has the same effect as PRINT, and it allows the program to accept information from the keyboard. Here's a simple example of a program that uses INPUT:

```
10 INPUT "HOW MUCH DO YOU WEIGH IN POUNDS";P
20 PRINT "YOUR METRIC WEIGHT IS"; P * .4534 "KILOGRAMS."
30 END
```

Line 10 flashes the question HOW MUCH DO YOU WEIGH IN POUNDS? on the computer's screen. A question mark isn't needed in the program, because INPUT automatically inserts it. The presence of the P after the semicolon tells the computer to stop and wait until someone enters his weight in pounds into the keyboard. After this keyboard entry is made, the weight in pounds is loaded into a memory location designated P. The computer then proceeds to line 20.

Line 20 tells the computer to display the words YOUR METRIC WEIGHT IS _____ KILOGRAMS. Everything inside quotation marks is automatically printed, and the semicolon tells the computer to print everything on the same line. P * .4534 introduces a couple of new ideas, however, so let's study them.

P is the label assigned to the memory location that stores your weight in pounds. The number .4534 is the conversion factor by which a weight expressed in pounds must be multiplied to get its metric equivalent in kilograms. And * is the BASIC symbol for multiplication. The usual multiplication sign, X, isn't used because it can be confused with a memory location by the computer or a programmer.

Now that you've seen how the program works, let's run it on the computer. Assume that the program is entered and that you've typed and entered RUN. The screen will display:

HOW MUCH DO YOU WEIGH IN POUNDS?—

This means that the computer is ready to receive your weight, so type in whatever your weight happens to be—our example uses 158. The screen will now display:

HOW MUCH DO YOU WEIGH IN POUNDS?158
YOUR METRIC WEIGHT IS 71.6372 KILOGRAMS.
READY
>

Impressed? This may not be very exciting with an imaginary computer, but it's very effective when tried on an actual computer in front of onlookers.

Here's another example of a program that uses INPUT to ask a question and PRINT to delivery a response:

```
10 INPUT "HOW MUCH MONEY DID YOU EARN LAST YEAR";M
20 PRINT "UNLESS YOU RECEIVE A SUBSTANTIAL RAISE, YOU WILL"
30 PRINT "HAVE TO WORK"; 1000000000/M; "YEARS TO EARN A"
40 PRINT "BILLION DOLLARS!"
50 END
```

You should have no trouble understanding how this program works, because we've introduced only two new BASIC rules. The first is that a long line of text can be split into a series of PRINT statements. The second is that BASIC uses the symbol / to indicate division.

Assuming your income last year was $15,000, here's what the screen will display after the program has been entered and run. You don't have to type in the dollar sign, because only the number of dollars— 15,000—matters in this program.

```
HOW MUCH MONEY DID YOU EARN LAST YEAR?15000
UNLESS YOU RECEIVE A SUBSTANTIAL RAISE, YOU WILL
HAVE TO WORK 66666.7 YEARS TO EARN A BILLION DOLLARS!
READY
>
```

Some conversational programs are amazingly complex, and can carry on almost human-like conversations. Many home computer enthusiasts enjoy developing such programs, just for the fun of showing people how smart their computers are.

An important BASIC operation that makes more advanced conversational programs possible is known as the *string function*. A string is simply a group of keyboard characters or symbols. It can be a sentence such as HOW ARE YOU?, a name, an address, a telephone number, or a list of characters such as (8 P?4S;+G.

A string is designated by the $ sign, and assigned to a memory location indicated by a letter of the alphabet. The number of strings you can use, and the number of characters in each string, depend on the type of computer you own. Some computers can accept only a couple of strings — A$ and B$, for instance — limited to a maximum number of characters. Other computers can assign a string function to any character of the alphabet, and can handle much longer strings.

The string function is very important in word processing, a computer application that is becoming increasingly popular.

PROGRAMMING FOR WORD PROCESSING

Word processing, either with special software for a home computer or with a business machine that

Word processing can be a writer's best friend. Corrections and revisions are much faster with word processing, and the final text can be stored on magnetic tape or disk. Take it easy—the computer does all the work.

doesn't do anything else, lets writers type their material directly into a computer. Mistakes can be corrected and revisions can be made much faster with word processing than with pencil and paper. And the final text can be stored on magnetic tape or disks that can be read by automatic typesetting equipment.

One very common use for word processing is generating "personalized" form letters. Here's a program for a form letter that a congressman's secretary can use to speed up answers to mail from constituents:

```
05 CLS
10 INPUT "WHAT IS THE VOTER'S TITLE AND LAST NAME";A$
20 INPUT "WHAT IS THE VOTER'S FIRST NAME ONLY";B$
30 PRINT
40 PRINT
50 PRINT "DEAR" ; A$; ":"
60 PRINT
70 PRINT "THANK YOU FOR YOUR LETTER, ";B$ "."
80 PRINT "I'M ALWAYS GLAD TO HEAR FROM VOTERS LIKE YOU."
90 PRINT "BE ASSURED I'LL TAKE YOUR VIEWS INTO ACCOUNT."
100 PRINT
110 PRINT                                    "REGARDS,"
120 PRINT
130 PRINT                                    "W.E. TAXMORE"
140 PRINT
150 PRINT
160 PRINT "IF YOU WANT TO PREPARE ANOTHER LETTER, TYPE RUN."
```

As you can see, this program is little more than a series of PRINT statements preceded by a couple of INPUT statements that assign the voter's full name and first name to two strings, A$ and B$.

Notice the space after "DEAR" in line 50? A space is needed here (and after LETTER in line 70) because strings are often placed directly adjacent to any text that's to be printed. The space inside the quotation marks makes certain that the letter's salutation will read "DEAR VOTER" and not "DEARVOTER."

Incidentally, look at the PRINT statements in lines 30, 40, 60, 100, 120, 140, and 150. These lines print nothing on the computer's screen. They simply skip lines to provide spaces in the final text. And the PRINT statements in lines 110 and 130 specify that the congressman's signature will appear at the right side of the letter, because space has been left after the PRINT and before the "REGARDS" and the signature. Otherwise, the signature would simply start a new line at the bottom of the letter.

Here's how the program is used to respond to Mr. Fed-up Taxpayer. First, the program asks for the constituent's name:

```
WHAT IS THE VOTER'S TITLE AND LAST NAME?MR. TAXPAYER
WHAT IS THE VOTER'S FIRST NAME ONLY?FED-UP
```

After the first name is entered, the screen displays the text of the personalized letter:

```
DEAR MR. TAXPAYER:

THANK YOU FOR YOU LETTER, FED-UP.
I'M ALWAYS GLAD TO HEAR FROM VOTERS LIKE YOU.
BE ASSURED I'LL TAKE YOUR VIEWS INTO ACCOUNT.

                                        REGARDS,

                                        W.E. TAXMORE

IF YOU WANT TO PREPARE ANOTHER LETTER, TYPE RUN.
READY
>
```

Of course, a printer is necessary to make full use of a computer's word-processing capabilities — these machines are discussed in Chapter 4, "Peripherals: Increasing Your Computer's Power." But think of all the applications you could find for a word-processing computer — personalized correspondence, mailing lists, record-keeping, and much more.

USING A COMPUTER AS A CALCULATOR

Now that we've seen how computers, especially personal ones, can be used for many jobs that have nothing to do with arithmetic, let's look at some of the more traditional roles they're used for.

A useful feature of the BASIC language used by many home computers is the so-called "calculator mode." You can try this mode out with your imaginary computer. Type:

PRINT 4 + 5

Then press ENTER. The screen instantly responds with:

9

The computer can also substract (−), multiply (*), and divide(/). For example:

PRINT 3 * 4 * 5 * 6

Then press ENTER. The screen will flash:

360

Here's another example. Type:

PRINT 123456/654321

Then press ENTER. The screen responds with:

.188678

Of course, you can easily perform all these operations with a pocket calculator. The computer only begins to outperform a calculator when it's used in its programming mode.

All of the BASIC operations we've already learned about, and several others, can be applied to programs involving numbers. Two new BASIC functions you should know about are READ and DATA, which are often used in arithmetic applications. Let's see how they work.

Using READ and DATA in Arithmetic Programs

READ is simple—it commands the computer to read the number in one or more designated memory locations. The numbers in the locations are supplied by DATA. Confused? Here's a simple program that shows how READ and DATA are used:

```
10 READ A, B
20 LET Q = A + B
30 LET S = A - B
40 PRINT Q/S
50 DATA 14, 63
60 END
```

After this program is entered and run, the screen of the computer will immediately display:

-1.57143

Do you understand how the program arrived at this value? Let's review the program a step at a time to make sure.

10 READ A, B

This READ statement tells the program to read the data stored in memory locations A and B in preparation for the next two steps.

20 LET Q = A + B

This step establishes a memory location identified as Q, and loads it with the sum of the numbers in locations A and B.

30 LET S = A - B

Another memory location, S, is established, and loaded with the difference between the numbers in A and B.

40 PRINT Q/S

This operation wraps up the program by dividing the number in Q by the number in S and flashing the result on the screen.

50 DATA 14, 63

Here's the data that's loaded into those memory locations A and B, described in line 10. The first number — 14 — is loaded into the first memory location (A), and the second number — 63 — is loaded into the second memory location (B). So A = 14 and B = 63.

How does the computer get to the data in time to use it when it's given at the end of the program?

Simple. Before it does anything else, the computer automatically reads any DATA statements that are in the program, no matter where they're located. It's customary to place DATA statements at the beginning or end of a program, but they can be placed anywhere; the computer will automatically find them.

READ and DATA are very useful, particularly because they let you use many different pieces of DATA in a program. But there's another way to supply numbers to a computer, too—INPUT.

Using INPUT In Arithmetic Problems

In the discussion about conversational programs earlier in this chapter, we learned how INPUT can be used by the computer to ask you the value of some variable, such as age or weight. INPUT can also be used to ask a series of questions, as in this revised version of the program that we looked at earlier:

```
10 INPUT "WHAT IS THE VALUE OF A";A
20 INPUT "WHAT IS THE VALUE OF B";B
30 LET Q = A + B
40 LET S = A - B
50 PRINT "A + B DIVIDED BY A-B IS";Q/S
60 GOTO 10
70 END
```

As you can see, this program eliminates the READ and DATA statements, and lets the computer simply ask for the information it needs. After the computer displays the result, line 60 loops the program back to the first line, and the computer asks the first question again.

Using FOR...NEXT in Number Applications

So far we haven't asked our imaginary computer to solve problems any more complicated than those a pocket calculator can easily handle. The FOR...NEXT operation, however, lets us write programs that order the computer to rapidly solve a series of problems and present the results in neatly tabulated rows on its screen — something no calculator can do.

For instance, here's a simple program that squares the numbers from 1 through 10 and displays the results:

```
10 FOR N = 1 TO 10
20 PRINT "THE SQUARE OF";N; "IS";N*N
30 NEXT N
40 END
```

Type RUN, press ENTER, and the screen will display:

```
THE SQUARE OF 1 IS 1
THE SQUARE OF 2 IS 4
THE SQUARE OF 3 IS 9
THE SQUARE OF 4 IS 16
THE SQUARE OF 5 IS 25
THE SQUARE OF 6 IS 36
THE SQUARE OF 7 IS 49
THE SQUARE OF 8 IS 64
THE SQUARE OF 9 IS 81
THE SQUARE OF 10 IS 100
```

Try that with a calculator! A calculator can easily square this sequence of numbers, of course, but it can't present the results in neatly tabulated form, complete with explanations. Only a computer can give you the answers like this.

Let's make the program fancier by having the computer display the numbers 1 through 10, their squares, their cubes, and their reciprocals (one divided by the number). Here's the new program.

```
10 PRINT "NUMBER", "SQUARE", "CUBE", "RECIPROCAL"
20 FOR N = 1 TO 10
30 PRINT N, N*N, N*N*N, 1/N
40 NEXT N
50 END
```

The commas in line 10 establish four columns, complete with titles. Line 30 supplies the information for the four columns. Run this program and the screen will display:

NUMBER	SQUARE	CUBE	RECIPROCAL
1	1	1	1
2	4	8	.5
3	9	27	.333333
4	16	64	.25
5	25	125	.2
6	36	216	.166667
7	49	343	.142857
9	64	512	.125
9	81	729	.111111
10	100	1000	.1

This should impress the most ardent calculator user—and it's only a trivial example of what can be done with the help of FOR...NEXT and PRINT.

Let's look at another example of how FOR...NEXT can be used. The following program generates the complete multiplication table for the digits 1 through 10, in less than three seconds:

```
05 CLS
10 PRINT "THE MULTIPLICATION TABLE"
20 PRINT
30 FOR X = 1 TO 10
40 PRINT X; " ";
50 NEXT X
60 PRINT
70 FOR Y = 2 TO 10
80 FOR Q = 1 TO 10
90 PRINT Y * Q; " ";
100 NEXT Q
110 PRINT
120 NEXT Y
130 GOTO 130
```

If programming appeals to you, why not spend a few minutes figuring out how this program works, using what you've learned so far? Remember, though, you don't have to know how a program works to use it. Programming can be fun—but if you don't enjoy it, don't get discouraged about using a computer. There's plenty of ready-to-run software available that doesn't require any programming at all.

COMPUTERS AS TEACHERS

As you've seen, computers can solve various kinds of arithmetic problems. They can even be programmed to teach people how to solve arithmetic problems.

Here's a very simple BASIC program that converts our imaginary computer into an electronic multiplication teacher:

```
05 CLS
10 LET R = RND (10)
20 LET Q = RND (10)
30 PRINT "WHAT IS";R; "TIMES";Q;
40 INPUT V
50 LET S = R*Q
60 IF S = V THEN 90
70 PRINT "SORRY, PLEASE TRY AGAIN..."
80 GOTO 30
90 PRINT "CONGRATULATIONS! THAT'S CORRECT."
100 PRINT "TYPE RUN IF YOU WANT TO TRY ANOTHER PROBLEM."
```

Here's sample run of this interesting program:

```
WHAT IS 7 TIMES 3?22
SORRY, PLEASE TRY AGAIN...
WHAT IS 7 TIMES 3?21
CONGRATULATIONS! THAT'S CORRECT.
TYPE RUN IF YOU WANT TO TRY ANOTHER PROBELM.
READY
>
```

Can you explain how the program works? Since you've already been introduced to all the BASIC statements used here, you should be able to figure it out. But again, it's not necessary to understand how the program works to use it. Even professional computer programmers often use programs developed by other people instead of writing their own.

A program like this can make learning the multiplication table fun. Teaching programs can be designed to present many different kinds of arithmetic problems. They can also be designed to teach facts— history, grammar, dates — and even foreign languages.

LEARNING MORE ABOUT PROGRAMMING

In this chapter, we've introduced many of the statements used for programming in BASIC. There are many other BASIC statements and operations, too, and you'll want to learn how they're used if you're interested in learning more about programming.

One area you'll want to cover is BASIC shortcuts. These are the tricks and abbreviations you can use to condense programs. Another is the use of subroutines — programs within a program — that are referred to over and over as the main program is being run by the computers.

You can find out more about BASIC from the dozens of books that have been published about this easy computer language. Because there are many dialects or versions of BASIC, it's important to look for books written for the version of BASIC used by

Once you've mastered the fundamentals of programming in BASIC, you can move on to BASIC shortcuts — tricks and abbreviations you can use to condense programs. Visit a computer store for some hands-on programming experience.

the computer you'll be working with.

You can learn the fundamentals of BASIC even if you don't have a home computer. For real hands-on experience, try visiting a computer store — many stores will be happy to let you try out some of the things you've learned here at the keyboard of a real computer. The members of a computer club are a good bet for giving you a trial session, too. Even if you don't think programming is for you, a brief session at the keyboard may surpise you. Give it a try— you'll discover that BASIC is very easy to learn.

The Vocabulary of BASIC

BASIC (Beginner's All-purpose Symbolic Instruction Code) is a high-level programming language used by most personal computers. There are more than 400 BASIC terms, commands, instructions, and symbols used by the 250 or so different kinds and models of computers that understand the BASIC computer language. No single computer understands every BASIC instruction, because there are different dialects of this computer language. But most computers understand a few dozen of the most important ones. Here are some examples of BASIC:

AUTO — A timesaver instruction that tells your computer to automatically assign a number for each line in your program; for example: 20 PRINT "BASIC IS A COMPUTER LANGUAGE."

BREAK—Allows you to interrupt a program that your computer is in the process of running. See CONT.

CLOAD—Used by some computers to load a program on a cassette tape into the computer's internal memory. See CSAVE.

CLS — Clear screen; a fast way to clear or erase everything from the computer's video screen. Very handy for quickly removing the text that can quickly fill up the screen of a video display.

CONT — Short for "continue." This command tells your computer to continue running the program you stopped by ordering a BREAK.

CSAVE—Used by some computers to load information or programs from the computer's internal memory onto a cassette tape. See CLOAD.

DATA—A statement that provides a handy place to put numbers or information intended for later readout by a READ command. The information should be separated by commas; for example, DATA 14, 27, 46. See READ.

DRAW—Used by some computers to permit a line to be drawn on a video screen. A similar command is called PLOT. Different computers require various information about the starting and ending points of the line to be drawn.

END—Placed at the end of a program, this is an instruction to your computer to stop and await further instruction. END isn't always needed, but it can prevent the computer from looking for something else to do because it hasn't been told to stop.

FOR-TO-NEXT — A powerful statement that allows you to cycle or loop through a section of your program as many times as you specify. For example:

```
10 FOR X = 1 TO 10
20 PRINT X * X
30 NEXT X
```

This simple example tells your computer to print out the square of each number from 1 through 10 on its screen.

IF-THEN—A conditional statement that tells your computer to jump ahead to another part of the program if a specific condition is met. For example:

```
IF X = 10 THEN 50
```

This instruction tells your computer to go to line 50 in your program if X — maybe the result of a previous operation — equals 10. Otherwise, the program will simply go on to the next line in the program.

INPUT—Tells your computer that it needs information from you, letting you respond to a programmed question. It can often be used in a program in place of PRINT, as in:

```
10 INPUT "HOW OLD ARE YOU";X
20 PRINT "YOU ARE";X
30 END
```

When you run this simple program, the computer will display on its screen HOW OLD ARE YOU?, even inserting the question mark. When you type in your age, the computer automatically assigns it to a special memory location labeled X. Then the computer will display YOU ARE, followed by whatever is in memory location X, in this case your age.

LET — In some older versions of BASIC, used to assign a value to a character or symbol, as in: LET Z = 100. LET is often optional, so the statement can be shortened to simply: Z = 100.

LIST — Entered from your keyboard, it tells the computer to display your program on its video screen.

PRINT — A command with many uses. PRINT can be used directly from your keyboard, as in: PRINT 1345 + 2078. The video screen will display 3423. PRINT can also be used as a statement in a program to print on the screen anything between quotation marks.

READ — Used with DATA, allows your program to assign information or numbers to their proper place.

REM — Short for "remark." Lets you identify your programs with helpful tags or labels and hints about their purpose and operation. REM statements take up valuable memory space, but they can save lots of frustration long after you've forgotten how to use a program you've saved for future use.

RUN — The go-ahead signal. When you type this into your keyboard, your computer will begin processing or running your program.

TAB — Similar to the tab key on a typewriter; used with PRINT statements to determine where information is to be printed on a line.

Chapter 7

What's on the way? Take a look at what's coming soon in the world of home computers—and in your world, too. You know what computers can do now. Don't miss this preview of how you'll be using them tomorrow!

The Future: What's Ahead in Computers?

ADVANCED ELECTRONICS has become an important part of our everyday lives — the century that began with the steam engine is ending with a technology that sends men into space, routinely. From calculators to solar-powered watches to video games, we're surrounded by the fruits of the computer revolution.

But even more amazing things are on the horizon — our sophisticated technology isn't standing still, it's moving ahead, with a speed that would dizzy Henry Ford. The home computer is considered by many people to be the most important consumer product since television, but it's only a prelude to what's to come.

CHARTING THE CHANGES

What is coming? Whatever the next century brings, the computer will be a part of it—and a big part. The "computer revolution" is more than just a catch phrase—it's a technological upheaval whose impact is as great as that of the Industrial Revolution. Computers, in fact, are not just another new tool. They're a completely new kind of tool — a tool that thinks. Wherever you live, whatever you do, computers are changing your life.

The Invisible Computer

Even if you never buy a home computer, machines that think are becoming a bigger and bigger part of your life. Microprocessors, the chips that are the brains of home computers, are rapidly finding their way into such common consumer items as microwave ovens, car engines, vending machines, and just about everything electronic. Most of these "invisible computers" operate entirely on their own; you may never even know they're there.

What do these microprocessors do? Besides making things easier to use — push a few buttons on a microwave oven to automatically defrost and cook your meal — one of their applications is saving energy. Besides microprocessor-controlled appliances that carefully control the amount of electricity used, one of the key applications of the future is the microprocessor-controlled car. Already silicon chips are used extensively in cars to control the carburetor and save fuel. Soon they'll automatically diagnose a car's problems; eventually, they'll help you plan a trip. The cars of the 1990s will probably have video screens, which, besides displaying such things as fuel capacity and speed, will even display a map of your trip and tell you where you are. Thanks to your car's invisible brain, getting around will be easier than ever.

The Shrinking Computer

One of the most exciting developments today is the arrival of the pocket computer. Far from being glorified calculators, these unique devices — just now beginning to become available—can do many of the things their full-sized counterparts can. The power that once existed only in room-size machines is being packed into smaller and smaller containers.

At the moment, pocket computers are rather limited and still rather expensive—about $300 to $500. Although they have miniature typewriter-like keyboards and understand BASIC, they don't have a great deal of memory, and they can display only one line of text at a time on a tiny liquid crystal display. But changes are in the wind. Computer scientists are packing more and more tiny circuits into fingernail-size chips. Couple these chips with the half-inch thick video display screens that should be available within the next few years, and you'll have all the computing power of big machines in a compact unit the size of a hardcover book—or even smaller.

For the short term, *portable* computers will become more popular. Larger than a pocket computer, these machines are still small enough to fit in a briefcase, and some have their own fold-up cases. Some models operate on batteries, others require an electrical outlet, but they're a long way from the huge boxes most of us think of when we hear the word "computer." Imagine commuting with a computer instead of an attache!

Computers are beginning to shrink in another way, too, and the pocket and portable models are an indication of what's ahead for all computers. This change is a simple one: peripherals, now plugged into a computer to expand its abilities, may eventually be absorbed into the computer itself. Modems and printers, among the most popular peripherals, may soon become standard parts of home computers. You won't have to buy add-ons to hook into a computer network or print copies of your programs; your computer will have a modem and a printer built in. Eventually, you may not need extra equipment to get many of the capabilities that are now provided by peripherals.

What's Happening to Prices

If you want to get your own home computer but you're afraid of radical changes in the market — remember how fast the price of calculators dropped?—don't let the promise of better things to come prevent you from joining the computer age right now. Even though today's $500 home computer gives you computer power that would have cost tens of thousands of dollars a decade ago, there's almost no chance that computers will become as inexpensive as pocket calculators.

The reason is simple: calculators have very few parts, and the price they sell for is very little more than the cost of those parts and the cost of labor to put them together. Home computers, on the other hand, have quite a few parts. The prices of today's home computers aren't expected to drop much more, because the cost of parts, labor, and distribution — getting them to your dealer's shelves—is pretty close to the price they sell for. The low end of the price range will probably stay at $300 to $500 for the foreseeable future.

Prices of computer accessories—peripherals—are declining, especially printers and floppy disk drives. But these prices too are starting to level off. Most pheripherals have quite a few parts, and there's a lot of labor involved in assembling them—especially if they contain moving parts.

The biggest cost reductions will come in larger computers and peripherals primarily designed for professional and business users. But home computers will stay at about the same price for some time to come.

THE FRIENDLY COMPUTER

"User-friendly" is one of the computer industry's hottest current catch-words. Computer salesmen will tell you about user-friendly software or a user-friendly computer. It's jargon, but all it means is that the machine doesn't require you to know much about computers to use it. Home computers *are* getting easier to use, although you still have to know which words to type into a keyboard to get the computer to do what you want it to do. And before you can use today's hardware, you have to read a manual. The same is true for the software.

Computer makers realize that more people will buy computers if they're easier to use, and they're already taking giant steps in this direction. Soon you'll see keyboards with separate buttons identified with plain English commands—like "copy," "load program," or "run program." There will also be more involved programs that will lead you step by step through everything you need to know to use them. There won't be any more long and boring manuals—everything will be simply displayed, right on the

It's getting easier all the time to be friends with your computer. Clear instructions right on the keyboard, step-by-step programs, no more boring manuals — it's all part of making computers "user-friendly."

screen in front of you. It won't be too long before anyone will be able to sit down at a computer and use it immediately, even if he's never seen a computer before.

Computers That Talk—And Listen

Someday you'll be able to sit down at your computer, give it a spoken command like, "Get me all recipes for chicken," and have it not only print out all the

Bad day at work? Problems with the family? Tell it to your personal computer. It's harder to get a computer to listen than to talk—but someday your computer will be able to obey spoken commands and talk back to you.

recipes, but also *tell* you vocally that it's looking. Remember the starship's computer on *Star Trek*? A voice said, "Working," every time Mr. Spock asked it for information. This kind of back-and-forth dialogue with a computer depends on two separate skills: the ability to talk, and the ability to listen. And as you might guess, the listening is harder.

Voice Recognition. Getting a computer to "understand" spoken words is extremely difficult. You'll see why if you think about spoken language for a few minutes. No two people sound alike, or even pronounce the same words in exactly the same way — think of the difference from New England to New Orleans! Some voices are high-pitched, some are low, and some say the same thing in different ways — for example, "Park the car," or "Take the automobile and place it in the marked space." Because a computer can't follow instructions unless every task is broken down into its simplest steps, too much information — or information expressed the wrong way — can overwhelm it.

The first step in getting a computer to understand voices is converting the sounds into the binary 1s and 0s the computer understands. This is relatively easy through the use of special circuits called A/D (analog/digital) converters, or ADCs. But after this the fun starts. Research is being done in two directions — getting the computer to analyze word meanings, and getting it to analyze actual sounds. But neither one is an easy task, and computers will have to have huge memories to understand more than just a few words.

Some plug-in boxes with microphones are available for hobbyists who want to experiment with voice recognition, but they're still very primitive, and have to be programmed specifically for your voice. They can still understand only a relatively few words. Although this whole field of interest is one of the hottest in computer science today, it will probably be well into the 1990s before there are computers that will truly "understand" when we tell them to do something.

Voice Synthesis. Getting a computer to talk, although it's not anywhere near as complicated as getting it to listen, is still difficult. A synthesized voice isn't merely a tape recording of someone's voice that's played back by the computer. Instead, voice synthesizers for computers work by analyzing the words you type in and breaking them down into the over 100 different individual sounds, called phonemes, spoken English is composed of. The computer generates a binary signal—the 1s and 0s it understands—for each phoneme, and feeds the signals to electronic circuitry that actually produces the sounds. Hopefully, what you end up with sounds like a human voice.

So far, voice synthesizers are still rather primitive. They have the metallic sound of robots in early science-fiction movies—there's no expression at all, just a flat, monotone sound. They're often hard to understand unless you listen very closely. More human-sounding voice synthesizers will be developed over the next few years, and you're likely to see them being built into more and more home computers. But there will always be video display screens and printers; it's still easier to read a list of items than to remember the same list told to you verbally.

If you're interested in experimenting with voice synthesis now, you can — there are various voice synthesizers available that plug into most home computers. These peripherals cost from $200 to $400, and sound far from natural—but they're fun to work with, and they'll give you a taste of the future. There are even some computer games being written to work with them.

Programming for Everyone

If you want to do your own programming now, you have to learn a programming language like BASIC and break down a task into individual steps. For example, a program to print the square root of all numbers from 1 through 100 its written like this:

```
10 CLS
20 FOR X = 1 TO 100
30 PRINT SQRT (X)
40 NEXT X
50 END
```

That's a very simple program in BASIC. Imagine instead that you could type this into your computer:

PRINT THE SQUARE ROOT OF NUMBERS FROM 1 TO 100.

Computer scientists are working hard on computer languages that will be so simple to use that anyone can write his own programs. Some simple versions already exist, although they're in the experimental stages and not generally available for home computers. These *conversational* programming languages should be available within the next five years, and probably won't be any more expensive than BASIC. Like BASIC, they'll come as standard equipment with home computers. How much easier could computing get?

THE CHANGING TECHNOLOGY

Computers are indeed becoming friendlier, and there's more reason for this than simple common sense. As we've stressed throughout this book, the technology is changing fast — both hardware and software have come a long way since the early days of computers. You shouldn't let this volatility keep you from getting involved with home computing, but you should be aware of what's in store for the future. Developments in both hardware and software over the next ten years will profoundly affect you and your lifestyle, much as the arrival of television did a couple of decades ago.

Advanced Microprocessors: Increasing the Brain Power

As scientists pack more and more circuits into the silicon chips used in computers, microprocessors—the brains of personal computers—will become more and more powerful. The 16-bit revolution is already seeming less revolutionary, because more sophisticated microprocessor chips are on the way. Already, major chip companies have built experimental microprocessors that handle data in 32-bit and even 64-bit chunks. When they become commercially available within the next five years, these microprocessors will have all the power of the multi-hundred-thousand-dollar computers now used by banks and large corporations. Although these microprocessors will be far from inexpensive at first—and will need more powerful peripherals—they'll eventually be cheap enough to bring big-computer power to everyone.

Advanced Memory: A Billion Bytes?

The key to making computers more powerful is adding memory—the more there is, the more the computer can do. Although most of today's home computers are limited to 64K of RAM (internal read/write memory), with some of the coming 16-bit machines able to handle up to 512K, future microprocessors will be able to handle even larger amounts. Some manufacturers are already working on chips that will hold over a million bytes of data!

Although RAM memory can be thought of as the actual working memory that the computer uses when it's running a program, the area of *mass storage*—like today's floppy disks—is even more important, because you must have some permanent means of storing data when the computer isn't turned on. There are a few important developments happening in that area right now.

Bubble Memory. So named because it stores information in microscopic magnetic bubbles, bubble memory can hold huge amounts of data in an extremely small space. Bubble memory was developed several years ago, but it's just now becoming inexpensive enough to consider for use in home computers. One Japanese computer firm is working on a computer that uses bubble memory in the form of plug-in cartridges the size of a matchbox. These

Bubble memory cartridges can store huge amounts of data, in microscopic magnetic bubbles.

small packages will hold even the largest programs in an easily portable form.

Bubble-memory cartridges have one disadvantage: they're faster than a cassette tape, but still much slower than a floppy disk. Although all-electronic, they don't have the random-access capabilities of a floppy disk, where the disk drive's head goes directly to the data it needs. Despite this drawback, bubble memory's ability to hold vast amounts of information in a small package means that it will be used in more computers in the future.

Optical Disks. Another form of mass data storage that holds promise for the future is a more sophisticated version of the laser-optical videodisc used to record movies and other entertainment. Some companies are developing special versions of the videodisk for use with computers. These new disks use microscopic light and dark areas to record the 1s and 0s of binary code. The information is read by a light beam instead of a record/play head—nothing physically touches the disk.

But the biggest advantage of video data storage is the huge amount of information that can be held on a single disk. A computer video disk can hold *billions* of bytes of data. To put that in some perspective, the entire *Encyclopedia Britannica* could be stored on a single disk!

One disadvantage of optical disks is that you can't erase information on them and record new data. Optical disks for computers will be *read/single-write* devices—a computer will be able to store information on them only once; they won't be reusable. You'll still need floppy disks for programs that require swapping information from computer to floppy disk and back again—but with optical disks, you'll be able to store an entire public library on your bookshelves.

Optical disks and disk players designed specifically for computers should start appearing within the next few years. It's too early to say exactly how much they'll cost, but the players should sell for less than $500, with disks costing about $20 to $30 each.

LOOKING AHEAD WITH HOME COMPUTERS

We've talked a lot about how computers themselves are changing — what's happening to hardware and software, and how new technology is changing the forms and expanding the uses of computers. But how will these new computers actually change your everyday life?

You're seeing some of the changes already, in the computer-controlled information network that every consumer is a part of. More far-reaching and exciting changes are sure to happen as the computer age goes on. The applications below are just a few of them.

Networks: The Computer Connection

Information utilities, which provide you with data by linking your computer through telephone lines to a large computer, will become increasingly important. Already, services like The Source, CompuServe, and Dow Jones News/Retrieval are providing data to thousands of information-hungry home computer owners.

To hook up to the huge central computers of these services, all you need is a modem — discussed in Chapter 4 — and access to a telephone line. Right now, you can get immediate information on everything from airline flight schedules to stock quotations or the latest news.

Nationwide telephone networks for home computers hold great promise for a "wired society."

Someday, exchanging electronic mail, messages, and programs with computer owners all over the country will become commonplace. Some information services already act as electronic mailboxes — it's as easy as making a phone call, and has the wide reach of a newspaper.

The telephone home computer connection will profoundly change the way we live. Already, some people are working at home on computer terminals rather than commuting to work every day. This

Will computers ever be able to think the way we do? Before we can build a machine that thinks like a human, we'll have to know how our own brains work — and so far, nobody really knows.

"telecommuting" has the potential for vast savings in energy and building costs — and, as a bonus, it also keeps families closer together. Telecommuting may become commonplace by the 1990s.

Artificial Intelligence?

Will computers ever think? Will we ever really see HAL, the computer in *2001: A Space Odyssey*? That question is the subject of a lively debate within the scientific community. The area of making computers "smarter" is called *artificial intelligence*. Research into this area has been going on for years, and some of the findings have already resulted in more user-friendly machines and easier-to-use programming languages.

A computer with true artificial intelligence would be able to "learn" — to take information you give it and make a decision based on its experience — prior information. Computers with at least a partial learning ability will exist by the year 2000. They'll probably be tied into a nationwide computer network, so that one computer will be able to ask another about a subject it has no information on.

But although such computers will seem to think, a true thinking machine with a will of its own is probably 50 years away — if it's ever built at all. The problem is that to build a machine that functions like a human brain, we have to understand how the human brain works—and we're still a long way from that.

Forging Ahead

Home computers have so many talents and possibilities that we've only begun to scratch the surface. By the end of this decade, the home computer will be a part of a home entertainment/control center. Instead of sitting on a desktop, your home computer will be hooked up to a nationwide telephone network, to optional disks, to your TV, and maybe to a video cassette recorder. You might even have a small satellite dish antenna on your roof or outside your window, for receiving information direct from orbiting satellites.

But more than playing a few games and keeping track of your household finances, the computer of the future will be hooked up to a climate-control and security system that will automatically turn your thermostat up and down, tell you how much electricity you've used today, and keep the house secure while you're away. You'll even be able to call your computer by telephone and ask it if everything's OK.

And that's not so far away! These applications are not science fiction. The technology to do them exists now — it's only waiting for someone to put it all together, and you can bet it won't be long. The computer age isn't just a possibility for the future; it's already here. Jump in and join the fun!

Bibliography: Selected Periodicals

Apple Orchard

Published bimonthly by International Apple Core, Inc.; 910 A George St., Santa Clara, CA 95050; single issue: $3.25; annual subscription: $15.

Apple Orchard, aimed at owners of Apple computers, isn't published by the Apple Computer Company, but by a federation of Apple computer user groups. A typical issue—about 110 pages—contains articles about peripherals designed for Apple computers, programs, programming languages, and how various parts of a computer work. There's also an extensive section devoted to new hardware and software products available for the Apple computer. Some of the contents may be too technical for beginners, but there's something here for every Apple owner.

BYTE

Published monthly by BYTE Publications, Inc.; 70 Main St., Peterborough NH 03458; single issue: $2.95; annual subscription: $19.

BYTE, the first magazine for computer hobbyists, has expanded from 96 pages to more than 500 pages each issue. Because it has very technical articles about both hardware and software, it's mostly for advanced computer users. It also has frequent product evaluations, owner's reports about computers and accessories, and hundreds of advertisements for computers, accessories, and software.

Creative Computing

Published monthly by Creative Computing; P.O. Box 789-M, Morristown, NJ 07960; single issue: $2.50; annual subscription: $20.

Creative Computing is written for the software enthusiast rather than for the hardware-oriented computer hobbyist. Software applications covered include computer art, music, artificial intelligence, speech synthesis, games, sports simulation, puzzles, investment analysis, and others. The magazine also includes product evaluations, fantasy, fiction, and social commentary.

Dr. Dobb's Journal

Published monthly by People's Computer Co.; 1263 El Camino Real, Box E, Menlo Park, CA 94025; single issue: $2.50; annual subscription: $25.

Dr. Dobb's Journal regularly publishes, in its own words, "joyful praise and raging complaints about vendors' products and services." In addition to product evaluations, it provides in-depth coverage of the software scene. It's definitely not a hardware-oriented magazine like BYTE and others, but may be too advanced for beginners.

Interface Age

Published monthly by McPheters, Wolfe & Jones; P.O. Box 1234, Cerritos, CA 90701; single issue: $2.50; annual subscription: $18.

Interface Age is similar to BYTE, with technical articles on both hardware and software, but it's simpler and easier to understand, with good graphics. It has fewer pages and ads than BYTE, but it's a good magazine for both beginning and more experienced computer users.

Microcomputing

Published monthly by Wayne Green, Inc.; 73 Pine St., Peterborough, NH 03458; single issue: $2.95; annual subscription: $25.

Microcomputing is a spin-off publication from the founder of BYTE, and it's very similar to BYTE, with technical articles on hardware and software. But this magazine is better organized, and articles are easier to find. Like BYTE, Microcomputing is a must for serious computer users.

Mini-Micro Systems

Published monthly by Cahner's Publishing Co.; 221 Columbus Ave., Boston, MA 02116; single issue: $4; annual subscription: $35.

Mini-Micro Systems is primarily intended for the professional who wants to stay abreast of the latest developments in small business computer systems. Many products described, however, are compatible with personal computers.

Nibble

Published eight times a year by MICRO-SPARC, Inc.; Box 325, Lincoln, MA 01773; single issue: $2.95; annual subscription: $19.95.

Nibble is a popular magazine among owners of Apple computers. Like *Apple Orchard*, it isn't published by the Apple Computer Company. A typical issue contains about 200 pages, including household, entertainment, and small-business programs, tips on programming, hardware construction projects, news, and reviews of products. The contents, entirely focused on Apple computer systems, seem to provide something for both beginners and advanced Apple users.

Personal Computing

Published monthly by Hayden Publishing Co.; P.O. Box 2941, Boulder, CO 80321; single issue: $2; annual subscription: $18.

Personal Computing is a well-illustrated, easy-to-understand magazine that gets high marks for its general contents. Aimed at computer users, a typical issue may include several BASIC programs, an article or two on how to make money with your computer, news about developments and products in personal computing, and perhaps a piece of fiction.

Popular Computing

Published monthly by BYTE Publications, Inc.; 70 Main St., Peterborough, NH 03458; single issue:

$2.50; annual subscription: $15.00.

Popular Computing is a general-coverage computer magazine that places emphasis on nontechnical subjects. In some respects, its content and language resemble Personal Computing. A typical issue will contain articles on word processing, programming, and new products. Columns include "Ask Popular," a forum that answers readers' general questions about small computers, as well as other columns having to do with specific applications; for example, "Small-Business Computing" and "Educational Computing."

80 Microcomputing

Published monthly by 1001001 Inc.; 80 Pine St., Peterborough, NH 03458; single issue: $2.95; annual subscription: $25.

80 Microcomputing is devoted entirely to users of Radio Shack's line of TRS-80 computers and accessories. The magazine contains many articles and advertisements about and for do-it-yourself and commercial TRS-80 accessories, too. Despite its coverage, the magazine isn't a Radio Shack mouthpiece; it's a must for serious TRS-80 users and owners.

Glossary

Acoustic coupler. A device that converts a computer's binary signals into audible tones, allowing the computer to send and receive information via the handset of an ordinary telephone. See Modem, Nonacoustic coupler.

Address. A specific location in a computer's memory that's used to store information. Addresses can be identified by binary numbers (machine language) or letters of the alphabet (a high-level computer language like BASIC).

ASCII code. An acronym for American Standard Code for Information Interchange, used to permit computers to remember and process words as well as numbers. ASCII is a binary code—a combination of 0s and 1s—for the upper- and lower-case letters of the alphabet, the 10 digits, various punctuation marks, and other symbols.

Assembly language. A low-level computer language that replaces the binary code of machine language that a computer understands with easily remembered, shorthand-style phrases, or memory aids — CLR for "clear," CVD for "convert to decimal," etc.— that people can understand.

BASIC. An acronym for Beginner's All-purpose Symbolic Instruction Code, an easily learned high-level computer programming language that's used to operate most personal computers.

Backup. A duplicate or extra copy of software made as a replacement in case of damage to or loss of the original.

Binary digit. A digit in the binary notation system; either 0 or 1. Commonly abbreviated *bit*.

Bit. Contraction for *binary digit*. A digital computer's smallest unit of information—either 0 or 1.

Bootstrap. A program, normally permanently stored in a computer's memory, used for starting the computer and getting it ready for use.

Bug. An error, defect, or problem. Software bugs are errors in programs or instruction manuals; hardware bugs are malfunctions in equipment.

Business computer. A computer designed specifically for commercial applications. Many personal computers can also be used for business applications.

Byte. A group of eight binary digits, or bits, that can indicate a number or character. One byte consists of two four-bit *nibbles*.

Cartridge. A plastic case containing one or more memory chips, and designed to be inserted or plugged into a receptacle in a computer. *See* Module.

Cassette. A plastic case containing two reels on which is wound a length of ⅛-inch magnetic recording tape. Cassettes used to record audio information can also record and store computer information for later use.

Central processing unit (CPU). The electronic nerve center of a computer, which commands the processing done by the computer. The CPU contains the arithmetic logic unit, as well as the control sections that retrieve program instructions from the memory, decode them, and then execute the instructions.

Chip. An integrated circuit. A tiny wafer of silicon measuring a few tenths of an inch square, on whose surface is etched and imprinted the hundreds or thousands of microscopic electronic components that comprise an integrated circuit. The chip is enclosed in a plastic or ceramic package for protection.

Circuit. An interconnected assortment of electronic components or integrated-circuit chips that together perform some useful operation.

Clock. An electronic circuit that emits a regulated sequence of electrical pulses synchronizing the operation of the many circuits in a digital computer.

Code. Any of numerous methods used to represent characters of the alphabet, numbers, punctuation marks, and other symbols with binary numbers.

Command. A character or word that orders a computer to do something.

Computer. A device that processes information. Analog computers process approximate information; digital computers process exact information.

Conditional. A program instruction that specifies an action such as a branch, or departure, to another part of the program if a specified condition is met.

Console computer. A desktop computer with a built-in video display screen.

Control section. An important part of a central processing unit (CPU). The control section is the network of electronic circuits that retrieves, decodes, and carries out programmed instructions in a computer.

Conversational programming. A method of programming a computer using ordinary English words and phrases. BASIC and other high-level languages can be used to develop conversational programs so that the computer can respond after each statement by the user.

CP/M. Control Program for Microprocessors; trademark. A popular operating system for small computers.

cps. An abbreviation for characters per second.

CPU. See Central processing unit.

CRT. An abbreviation for cathode-ray tube, the video display tube used in television sets, terminals, radar displays, and video monitors.

Cursor. A movable indicator on the screen of a video display that shows where the next character or symbol will appear.

Daisy wheel. A typing element, or print wheel, for an

impact printer that produces fully formed, high-quality characters. The characters on the daisy wheel take the form of raised outlines at the ends of spokes extending from the element's central axis, much like the petals of a daisy.

Data. Usually refers to numerical information, but may mean any kind of information put into and retrieved from a computer. DATA is also a BASIC computer language statement that precedes one or more pieces of numerical information in a program.

Data base. An organized collection of information that can be accessed by a computer.

Data processing. What a computer does when it sorts, manipulates, rearranges, and otherwise processes information.

Debugging. The sometimes lengthy and often tedious procedure of troubleshooting and eliminating errors in software or malfunctions in hardware.

Decision. A computer operation that compares two pieces of information or verifies a single piece of information, and then takes a specified action.

Decode. The process by which the central processing unit interprets instructions stored in a computer's memory.

Desktop computer. A computer small enough to fit on the top of a desk. Often the computer is installed inside the keyboard assembly, which is connected to a video monitor by means of a short, flexible cable.

Digital computer. An electronic system that represents numbers, symbols, and characters with binary numbers (0s and 1s) and processes such information according to a list of instructions stored in memory.

Disk. A flat, phonograph-record-like metal or plastic disk coated with a magnetic substance and used to store information; made in various sizes. Flexible plastic disks are called floppy disks. See *also* Magnetic disk memory.

Disk drive. A motorized device that spins a magnetic disk at high speed. The drive contains a sensing device that can both read information from and write onto the surface of the disk in the form of magnetized patterns.

Diskette. A floppy disk. See Floppy disk, Magnetic disk memory.

Disk memory. See Magnetic disk memory.

Documentation. Operating instructions, applications information, servicing information, programs, and other forms of software supplied with a computer or available separately.

Dot-matrix printer. See Matrix printer.

Dumb terminal. A video display unit and keyboard that can communicate with a computer, but that cannot on its own perform computer operations. See Smart terminal.

Electronic mail. A method of transmitting information over ordinary telephone lines. Often a pair of computers can be used to transmit correspondence and other communications between each other.

Erase. To remove or clear information stored in a computer's memory.

Execute. To perform a specified operation listed in a program, or to run the entire program.

Floppy disk. A flexible magnetic disk made from plastic and coated with a magnetic material. See Magnetic disk memory.

Glitch. An unwanted and undesirable electrical pulse inside a digital computer, which can cause errors in a program. A glitch may occur because of improper design, or it may find its way into the computer via power lines or even through the airwaves.

Handheld computer. A compact computer that can be held in one hand.

Hard copy. Computer output — programs, information, results, and other data — printed on paper by a printing device connected to the computer; a document.

Hardware. Keyboards, video monitors, memory storage devices, circuit boards, and all other electronic circuits and physical equipment that form a computer or computer system.

High-level language. A computer language in which each instruction or statement represents several binary code instructions in machine language. High-level languages allow computer users to write in terms that are familiar to them. For example, BASIC uses English words to instruct the computer. See *also* Machine language.

Impact printer. A printer that forms characters or symbols by striking a hammer or printhead against a carbon or inked ribbon and a sheet of paper. Some impact printers form a character in a single operation; others form characters from patterns of dots. See *also* Nonimpact printer.

Ink-jet printer. A type of nonimpact printer that forms characters by squirting a tiny jet of ink onto paper. The jet is directed by a magnetic field controlled by electronic circuits in the printer. See Impact printer.

Input/output device. Computer equipment used both to load information into a computer and to read information from the computer.

Input peripheral. Any device designed to transfer information into a computer. For example, keyboards and joysticks are input peripherals. *See also* Output peripheral.

Instruction set. The collection of various instructions that a particular computer can understand.

Integrated circuit (IC). A microminiature electronic circuit that's imprinted and etched on the surface of a silicon chip. *See also* Chip.

Interface. The linkage between two parts of a computer or between a computer and an accessory.

Interrupt. A temporary and often brief interruption in the execution of a program so that a digital computer can handle or service an external event such as the printing of a character.

Joystick. A movable shaft that permits positional information to be transferred into a computer. Used most often to move animated figures and missiles around the screens of game-playing computers, joysticks have more serious roles as well. For example, a joystick can be used to move an arrow or marker around the screen of a computer to assist in editing a program or designing graphics patterns.

K. A common way of describing the memory capability of a computer. K is derived from the prefix *kilo-*, and means approximately 1000 information units. An exact definition of K is 2^{10} or 1024 bytes. Therefore, an 8K computer memory can store 8192 pieces of information.

Keyboard. An array of keys, buttons, or switches that permit instructions and numerical information to be entered into a computer manually.

Language. An organized system of words, phrases, symbols, characters, and numbers that permits a computer operator to communicate with the computer. *See also* Assembly language, BASIC.

Light pen. A probe-like device, containing a light-sensitive cell at the tip, which, when pointed toward a video display screen, allows the computer to compute the location and know precisely where the probe is being aimed. The light pen can be used to make data selections on the video screen.

Line. A line of information in a computer program.

Line printer. A type of impact or nonimpact printer that produces a complete line of print in one high-speed operation.

Loop. A sequence of one or more computer instructions in a program that are executed repeatedly until one or more specified conditions have been met.

Machine. A microcomputer.

Machine language. A computer's native language of binary numbers (0s and 1s); the internal binary language into which a more advanced programming language must be converted before a computer can process a program.

Magnetic bubble memory. A specialized solid-state memory, made from high-density semiconductors, that stores information in the form of microscopic magnetic regions on a thin wafer of garnet. When viewed through a special microscope, the magnetic regions resemble bubbles. These regions can be moved through the crystal in which they're formed by means of a magnetic field.

Magnetic disk memory. A computer memory that records binary information on disks of various diameters, made of metal or plastic and coated with a magnetized substance. Information is read from and written on the magnetic surface of the disk with a recording head similar to those used in tape recorders.

Magnetic tape memory. A computer memory that records binary information on magnetic recording tape.

Mass storage media. Material such as magnetic tape and disk memories that stores enormous quantities of information in a relatively small space.

Matrix printer. A printer that forms characters from patterns of closely spaced dots.

Memory. The circuits, components, or mechanical portions of a digital computer that store information.

Menu. A list of choices displayed by a computer program, from which the user may select an option.

Micro. A microcomputer.

Microcomputer. A digital computer that uses a microprocessor for a central processing unit. Nearly all personal computers are microcomputers. *See also* Microprocessor, Central processing unit.

Microprocessor. A tiny integrated circuit that contains the complete central processing unit for a small digital computer. A microcomputer is made by connecting a memory integrated circuit to a microprocessor. *See also* Chip.

Minifloppy. A flexible plastic magnetic disk memory, about 5¼ inches in diameter. *See also* Magnetic disk memory.

Modem. An acronym for modulator-demodulator, a device that permits computers to communicate with one another, often over telephone lines. *See also* Acoustic coupler, Nonacoustic coupler.

Module. A plastic case with one or more memory chips, designed to be inserted or plugged into a receptacle in a computer. *See also* Cartridge.

Music synthesizer. An electronic circuit that can synthesize (create) musical sounds. Some personal computers can be programmed to simulate the operation of a music synthesizer.

Network. An arrangement for interconnecting a number of computers by telephone lines or other direct means.

Nibble. A common reference to a binary number or word composed of four bits; half a byte. *See also* Bit, Byte.

Nonacoustic coupler. A device that connects a computer directly to a telephone line. It converts a computer's binary signals into audible tones to allow the computer to send and receive information via a telephone line. *See also* Modem.

Nonimpact printer. A printer that forms characters without striking a carbon or inked ribbon against paper. For example, the thermal printer is a nonimpact printer that forms characters by heating patterns of dots on heat-sensitive paper. Nonimpact printers are much quieter than the impact variety. *See also* Impact printer, Ink-jet printer.

Nonvolatile. A term used in reference to a computer memory that stores information with or without electrical power. When the electrical power is turned off, the information stored is not lost. Common examples of nonvolatile memories include magnetic tape and disks.

Output peripheral. Any device designed to receive information or signals from a computer. Video monitors and printers are common output peripherals. *See also* Input peripheral.

Peripheral. Any input or output circuit or device designed to be connected to a computer.

Personal computer. A home computer. A low-cost microcomputer equipped with an input mechanism such as a typewriter-like keyboard and an output device such as a video monitor or printer.

Plotter. A device that produces an inked drawing of graphics patterns or text, or both. The pen that makes the drawing is moved across paper by means of a motor-and-pulley arrangement.

Power supply. The electronic circuits that convert power from an electrical outlet into a form suitable for use by a computer.

Printer. A device that prints programs, results of programs, and other information on either individual sheets or continuous strips of paper. *Impact printers* print by striking an embossed mechanism or array of pins against a carbon or inked ribbon next to the paper. *Nonimpact printers* print by applying heat or electricity to specially prepared papers.

Processor. A digital computer.

Program. The set or list of instructions that instructs a computer what to do and how to do it. *See also* Software.

Prompt. A message from a computer informing its user about an error or advising the user to take some action.

RAM. An acronym for *random-access memory*. See Random-access memory.

Random-access memory (RAM). A computer memory, often a solid-state integrated circuit, that stores and recalls information in any order or sequence. Unlike read-only memories (ROMs), RAMs require electrical power to remember information; turn off the power and the information is lost. See also Read-only memory.

Read. The process of retrieving information from a circuit, memory chip, punched tape, or magnetic tape or disk. The original information is not altered.

Read-only memory (ROM). A computer memory, often a solid-state integrated circuit, that stores permanent information that cannot be erased and changed or lost even if electrical power is turned off. See also Random-access memory.

Read-write memory. A computer memory such as magnetic tape or a disk used to store information, or an integrated circuit whose contents can be erased and changed. Because semiconductor read-write memories are random-access devices, they are often called RAMs. See Random-access memory.

RF modulator. An electronic circuit that permits a computer to be connected directly to an ordinary television set to provide a video display.

ROM. An acronym for read-only memory. See Read-only memory.

Run. To begin the execution of a computer program.

Semiconductor. The crystalline substance used to make memory chips, microcomputer chips, and other integrated circuits. The most common semiconductor for these purposes is silicon, the principle ingredient of ordinary beach sand. See Chip and Integrated Circuit.

Smart terminal. A keyboard and video display assembly that's capable of performing computer-like operations. It's primary role, however, is communicating with a true computer. See also Dumb terminal.

Software. A collective term for programs, lists, operating instructions, and other documentation, associated with the operation of a computer.

Solid-state. A reference to electronic components or complete circuits made from silicon, germanium, or other solid substances.

Statement. A line in a computer program; for example, PRINT A.

Store. To remember a piece of information.

Subroutine. One or more sequential instructions in a computer program that are ordinarily used more than once by the program. Subroutines may be as brief as several lines or they may be considerably longer than the main program that includes them. See also Branch.

Terminal. An input or output device connected to computer, capable of sending and receiving information. A terminal is usually an input device like a keyboard and an output device such as a video display unit or a printer.

Thermal printer. A nonimpact printer that forms

characters by making blue or black dots on heat-sensitive paper. The paper contains tiny microcapsules of ink that are burst open by heat from the thermal heating elements of the print mechanism.

Variable. In the BASIC computer language, a variable is a letter of the alphabet assigned to a memory location that can contain any designated number.

VDT. An abbreviation for video display terminal. *See also* CRT.

Video graphics. Diagrams, charts, graphs, figures, drawings, and patterns formed on a video screen. Computers with considerable memory can produce moving graphics patterns. Graphics have many recreational applications, but they were originally developed and are still used for commercial applications.

Video monitor. The television-like device on which computer information in the form of text or graphics is displayed on a screen.

Voice synthesizer. An electronic circuit that simulates the human voice, usually under the control of a ROM. *See also* ROM.

Volatile. A term used in reference to a computer memory that requires electrical power to retain information. Most RAMs used in personal computers are volatile; turn off the electrical power to the computer and any information in the RAM is lost.

Word. A common reference to a sequence of bits, often an 8-bit byte, that represents a number, symbol, letter of the alphabet, or program instruction. Personal computer words are usually 8 bits in length. Some newer computers use 16-bit words (two bytes).

Word processing. A method of using a computer as an electronic typewriter with a built-in memory. Word processing speeds up the preparation of error-free text. It also permits efficient editing, the storage on magnetic disks of correspondence and other information, and simplified preparation of mailing lists.

Word processor. An automated, computer-based system for producing typed documents.

Write. To store information in a memory chip or a punched tape, or on a magnetic tape or disk.

Index

A

Acoustic Coupler.
  See Modem, Acoustic
A/D converters, 42, 211
Address, definition of, 226
Analog/Digital Converters.
  See A/D converters
Apple, 145–48, 221, 224
  memory expansion of, 119
Apple Disk II floppy disk drive, 147
Apple Orchard magazine, 221
Apple Silentype printer, 147
Apple II, 145–47
Apple III, 147–48
Applications software programs, 56
Artificial intelligence, 219
Assembly language, 53
Atari, 140
  400, 142
  410 cassette tape recorder, 141, 143
  800, 140
  810 floppy disk drive, 141
  825 printer, 141
  830 acoustic modem, 141
AUTO command, 199

B

BASIC (Beginner's All-purpose
   Symbolic Instruction Code), 37,
   55–56, 126, 168, Chapter 6, 227
 vocabulary of 199–202
Binary digit, definition of, 227
Binary numbering system, 29, 52–53
Bit (binary digit), 29, 227
Bootstrap programs, 37
BREAK key, 174, 181, 199
Bubble memory, 215–16
Bug, definition of, 50, 227
Business software, 71–73
Business uses of personal computers,
   18, 71–72
Byte magazine, 222
Byte, definition of, 30, 227

C

Cartridge, plug-in, 66–67, 227
   Texas Instruments Command
   Modules, 136
Cassette tape, 60–62.
 See Also Cassette tape recorders, 47,
   60, 82–83
   Atari 410, 143
   Radio Shack CTR-80A, 138
   Radio Shack Minisette-9, 150
   Sharp CE-152, 150
   speed of, 61
Central Processing Unit (CPU),
   definition of, 227
Chip, definition of, 228
Circuit, definition of, 228
CLS (clear screen) command, 179, 182
COBOL (COmmon Business Oriented
   Language), 53–54
Code, definition of, 228
Commodore, 131–35
   CBM, 134

    Model 64, 133
    PET, 131
    SuperPet, 135
    VIC 1515 printer, 132
    VIC 1600 modem, 133
    VIC-20, 131–33
CompuServe, 20, 217
Computer
  calculator, 190
  camps, 23
  clubs, 75
  building your own, 162
  buying used, 159
  cost of, 11
  definition of, 7, 228
  documentation for, 128
  educational uses, 15, 196
  factors in purchasing, 121–28
  future uses of, 204–8
  games, 17, 69
  handheld, 149–54
  home uses of, 11–23
  kits, 162
  languages, 50–56
  model descriptions, 129–48
    Apple II, 145
    Apple III, 147
    Atari 400, 142
    Atari 800, 140
    Commodore CBM, 134
    Commodore Model 64, 133
    Commodore PET, 131
    Commodore SuperPet, 135
    Commodore VIC-20, 131
    IBM personal computer, 143
    Quasar/Panasonic HHC, 152
    Radio Shack Model 16, 140
    Radio Shack TRS-80, 137
    Radio Shack TRS-80 Model II, 140
    Radio Shack TRS-80 Model III, 139
    Radio Shack TRS-80 PC-2, 149

 Sharp PC-1500, 149
 Texas Instruments TI 99/4A, 135
 Timex/Sinclair 1000, 129
 Timex/Sinclair Spectrum, 131
prices of, 207
repair service, 156, 158
stores, buying at, 157
types of, 10
versus calculator, 7
where to buy, 154–63
Conditional transfer statement, 174
Console computer, definition of, 208
Control section, definition of, 208
Controller, Texas Instruments PHP 1800, 137
Conversational programming, 184, 213, 229
Copy Protection, 77
CP/M (Control Program for Microprocessors), 58
cps, definition of, 229
CPU. See Central Processing Unit
Creative Computing magazine, 222
CRT (cathode ray tube), 229.
 See also Video display
Cursor, 40, 170, 229
 control keys, 40

D

Daisy wheel printers.
 See Printers, impact, fully formed character
Data, 7, 29, 229
Databases, 20
Database managers, 71
DATA command, 191, 200
Data processing, definition of, 229
DATA statements, 200
Debugging, definition of, 229
Department stores, 155

Desktop computers, 10, 230
 See also Computer, individual
    model descriptions
Digital computer, definition of, 230
Direct-connect modem.
 See Modem, direct-connect
Directory, 84
Disk drive controller, 83, 91
Disk drives, 230
 floppy, 47, 63, 83
   advantages of, 84
   Apple Disk II, 147
   Atari 810, 141
   components of, 83
   density of, 88
   disadvantages of, 87
   IBM system unit, 143
   head cleaning kits, 91
   how to buy, 87
   number needed, 90
   Texas Instruments PHP 1850, 137
 types of, 88–93
Diskette, definition of, 230
Disk, 230
 floppy, 230
   data capacity of, 89
   copying, 90
   density of, 88
   sizes of, 64
 hard, 64, 91
   cost of, 93
   data capacity, 93
 optical, 216
Disk operating system, 58, 83
Division, 186, 190
Documentation, 128, 231
DOS (Disk Operating System), 58, 83
Dot-matrix printers.
 See Printers, dot-matrix
Dow Jones News/Retrieval, 15, 217
Dr. Dobb's Journal (magazine), 223

Dumb terminal, 231

E

Education and computers, 15–17, 196
Educational software, 71
80 Microcomputing magazine, 225
Electronic mail, 20, 109, 231
END *command,* 172, 174, 200
ENTER *command,* 170
Erase, definition of, 231
Execute, definition of, 231
Expandability, 122
  Apple circuitry, 145

F

Fan-fold paper, 103
File, 63
Floppy disks, 231.
  See Disk drives, floppy
FOR...NEXT command, 181, 194
FORTRAN (FORmula TRANslation), 54
Fully formed character printers.
  See Printers, impact

G

Games, 17, 69–70
GOTO command, 173
Graphics keys, 40

H

Handheld (pocket) computers, 10, 149–54, 231
Hard copy, 93, 232
Hard disk drives.
  See Disks, hard
Hard disks.
  See Disks, hard
Hardware, Chapter 2; 9, 26, 232
Hardware, versus software, 26, 49

Heath Company, 162
High-level language, 53, 232
  See also Computer languages
Household finances and computers, 14
Household software, 70–71

I

IBM Personal Computer, 143–45
IF...THEN command, 174, 177, 201
Impact printers, 232.
  See Printers, impact
Ink-jet printer, 232.
  See Printers, nonimpact
  INPUT command, 201, 184, 193
Input, 8
Input devices, 8, 37–42
  See also Peripherals
Input/output devices, 47
Input peripheral, definition of, 232
Instruction manuals, 75
Integrated circuit (IC), definition of, 233
Interface Age magazine, 223
Interface, definition of, 233
  See also Parallel interfaces, Serial interfaces
Investments and computers, 14–15

J

Joystick, 42, 109, 233

K

"K," definition of, 33, 233
Keyboard, 38–40, 233
  membrane, 130
Keypad, 40
Kits, 162

L

Language, definition of, 234
  See also Computer languages
LET command, 176, 201
Letter-quality printers.
  See Printers, impact
Light pens, 115–16, 234
Line filter, 116
LIST command, 172, 212
Loop, definition of, 173, 234

M

Machine language, 52, 234
Magnetic bubble memory, 215, 234
Magnetic media, 59–67
  See also Cassette tape, Disks
Mail-order buying, 156–57
Manufacturers
  back-up policies, 78
  reputation, 128
Mass storage, 216
Matrix printer, definition of, 235
Membrane keyboard, 130
Memory, 8, 31–37, 126, 214, 235
  bubble, 215–16
  capacity, 118
  expansion, 118–19
    cost of, 119
    methods of, 119
  size of, 33–36
  types of, 31
Menu, definition of, 235
Micro, definition of, 235
Microcomputer, 235
  See also Computer
Microcomputing magazine, 223
Microprocessor, 7, 28–31, 205, 214, 235
Minifloppy, 88, 236
  See also Disks, floppy

Mini-Micro Systems magazine, 223
Modem (modulator/demodulator), 20, 109
 acoustic, 110
  Atari 830, 141
  Commodore VIC 1600 VICMODEM, 133
 direct-connect, 110
 prices, 111
  Quasar/Panasonic RL-P4001, 154
  Texas Instruments PHP 1600, 137
 future of, 207
Module, definition of, 236
 See also Cartridges
Monitor.
 See Video display
Music synthesis, 46, 236

N

Network, 217
Nibble magazine, 224
Nibble, definition of, 30, 236
Nonacoustic coupler, definition of, 236
 See also Modem, nonacoustic
Nonimpact printers, 236.
 See Printers, nonimpact
Nonvolatile memory, 37, 237

O

Operating system, 56–59
Optical disks.
 See Disks, optical
Output, 8
Output devices, 46
Output peripheral, definition of, 237

P

Panasonic.
 See Quasar/Panasonic

Parallel interfaces, 106
Peripherals, Chapter 4; 10, 81, 126–27, 237
  See also AD converters, Cassette tape recorders, Disk drives, Joystick, Light pen, Memory expansion, Modem, Plotter, Power protector, Printers
  future of, 207
Personal computer, definition of, 10, 237
Personal Computing magazine, 224
Piracy, See Software, piracy of
Plotter, 116, 237
Pocket computers, 206
  See also Computer, handheld
Popular Computing magazine, 224
Portable computers, 11, 206
Power protectors, 116–18
PRINT command, 171, 202
Printers, 46, 93–109, 237
  character per line capacity, 104
  Commodore VIC 1515, 132
    Atari 825, 141
  factors in choosing, 102–07
  friction feed, 103
  future of, 207
  graphic, 42
    Sharp CE-150, 150
  impact, 95–98, 232
  dot-matrix, 98–100
    Texas Instruments PHP 2500, 137
  fully formed character
    daisy wheel, 95
    speed of, 96
    thimble, 97
  interfaces, 105
  matrix sizes, 105
  nonimpact
    electrographic dot-matrix, 100–1
    ink-jet, 101–2, 232

   laser, 102
   thermal dot-matrix, 100
   Apple Silentype, 147
   Quasar/Panasonic RL-P1003, 153
  paper, 103
  paper feed mechanism, 103
  pin feed (tractor feed), 103
  prices of, 94, 107–9
  Radio Shack Model VII, 138
  ribbons, 102
  special features, 106
  speed of, 96, 104
  type styles, 104–5
  warranties, 107
Printhead, 94
Processor, 8, 238
Program, 7, 60, 238
Programming, Chapter 6; 198
  conversational, 184
  future, 212
  languages. See Computer languages
Prompt, 176, 238

Q

Quasar/Panasonic
  HHC, 152
  RL-P1003 printer, 153
  RL-P4001 modem, 154

R

Radio Shack, 137–40
  CTR-80A cassette recorder, 138
  Disk Drive Kit 1, 139
  Minisette-9 cassette tape recorder, 150
  Model 16, 140
  TRS-80, 137
  TRS-80 Color Computer, 137
  TRS-80 Model II, 140
  TRS-80 Model III, 139
  TRS-80 PC-2, 149

RAM. *See* Random Access Memory
Random-access device, 84
Random Access Memory, 32–36, 50, 118, 126, 214
Read-only memory, 36, 50, 66, 239
Read-write memory, definition of, 238
REM command, 202
RF modulator, 43, 239
ROM. *See* Read Only Memory
Run, definition of, 239

S

Semiconductor, definition of, 239
Serial interfaces, 106
Service. *See* Computer, repair service
Sharp
  CE-150 printer, 150
  CE-152 cassette tape recorder, 150
  PC-1500, 149
Sinclair ZX-81, 129
6502 microprocessor, 29
Smart terminal, definition of, 239
Software, Chapter 3; 9, 26, 127, 239
  business, 71–73
  educational, 71
  free copies of, 76
  games, 69–70
  household, 70–71
  how to buy, 73–74
  media, 59–67
  packages, 50
  personal library of, 74
  piracy of, 77–78
  prices of, 74
  types of, 67–73
  versus hardware, 26–28, 49
  word processing, 73
Source, The, 20
Speaker, 46
Speech synthesis, 137
String function ($), 186

Subroutines, 93, 198, 240
System unit, 143

T

Telecomputing, 20–21, 109–15, 217–19
 See also Modem, Network
Terminals, 47, 112–15, 240
 dumb, 112, 231
 prices, 112–14
 smart, 112, 239
Texas Instruments, 135–37
 PHP 1800 disk controller, 137
 TI 99/4A, 136
Thermal printers, 240.
 See Printers, nonimpact
Thimble wheel.
 See Printers, impact
Time-sharing, 113
Timer, 182
Timex/Sinclair, 129–31
 1000, 129
 Spectrum, 131
Typesetting, 188

U

Unconditional transfer statement, 174
Uninterruptable power supply, 117
Universal Product Code (UPC), 59
UPS. See Uninterruptable power supply
Used computers, 159
User groups. See Computer, clubs
User-friendliness, 126
 future of, 208

V

VDT, (video display tube), 240.
 See Video display
Video display, 43

factors in selecting, 126
Video graphics, 240.
Video modulator, 137
Video monitor, 240.
 See also Video display
Voice recognition, 42, 210
Voice synthesis, 47, 211
Volatile memory, 33, 241.
 See also RAM

W

Warranties, 107, 128, 160
Winchester disk drives. See Disks, hard
Word processing, 18, 73, 187, 241
Word processor, definition of, 241

Z

Z-80 microprocessor, 29